Essential
Food & Drink
SPAIN

by
PEPITA ARIS

Pepita Aris is a cookery writer and editor
who has had a house in Spain for 20 years.
Author of *Recipes from a Spanish Village*, she
is a magazine contributor and broadcaster on
Spanish food.

D0273381

Produced by the Publishing Division of
The Automobile Association

Written by Pepita Aris
Consultant: Bridget Jones
Copy Editors: Barbara Croxford,
Audrey Horne

Edited, designed and produced by
AA Publishing.
© The Automobile Association 1992.
Map © The Automobile Association
1992.

Reprinted 1994 and 1995

Distributed in the United Kingdom
by AA Publishing, Norfolk House,
Priestley Road, Basingstoke,
Hampshire, RG24 9NY.

A CIP catalogue record for this book
is available from the British Library.

ISBN 0 7495 0438 2

The contents of this publication are
believed correct at the time of
printing. Nevertheless, the
publishers cannot be held
responsible for any errors or
omissions or for changes in the
details given in this guide or for the
consequences of any reliance on the
information provided by the same.

We have tried to ensure accuracy
in this guide, but things do change
and we would be grateful if
readers would advise us of any
inaccuracies they may encounter.

Published by AA Publishing, a
trading name of Automobile
Association Developments Limited,
whose registered office is Norfolk
House, Priestley Road, Basingstoke,
Hampshire, RG24 9NY.
Registered number 1878835.

Typesetting: Microset Graphics Ltd,
Basingstoke

Colour separation: Scantrans P.T.E.,
(Singapore)

Printed by: Printers Trento, S.R.L.,
Italy

Front cover picture: Alcachofas
salteadas con jamón

ABOUT THIS BOOK   4

INTRODUCTION   5

THE REGIONS OF SPAIN   7

A–Z GUIDE TO
SPANISH FOODS   17

WINES OF SPAIN   76

A–Z OF DRINKS   83

SHOPPING   91

RECIPES   98

SPECIAL EVENTS   114

EATING OUT   115

CHILDREN   120

SPECIAL DIETS   121

TIGHT BUDGET   121

PRACTICAL TIPS   122

LANGUAGE   123

NOTES ON USING THE
RECIPES   126

INDEX   127

This book employs a
simple rating system for
dishes and specialities in
the A–Z sections on foods
and drinks:

◆◆◆   something really
      special

◆◆   try it if you can

◆   worth a try if you
      come across it

ABOUT THIS BOOK

One of the pleasures of travelling is sampling the local food and drink. Whether your tastes are adventurous or conservative, this book will whet your appetite and give you a genuine taste of Spain. The perfect companion to any meal, it may change your ideas about what is on offer – it is not all tapas and paella.

Not only will this book help you to appreciate the true flavours of the country, the practical information will enable you to cope with new or unfamiliar situations, taking the worry out of getting what you want.

Spain's regions are colourfully described, with the emphasis on local foods and specialities, and a look at the influences and traditions that you can still detect in them.

A comprehensive A–Z covers both the foods you are likely to see in shops and markets and the dishes on menus, with star ratings to help you make choices. Where items in this list appear elsewhere in the text, they are printed in small capitals, thus: GAZPACHO.

There is information and advice on wines; along with an A–Z of other drinks, both alcoholic and non-alcoholic, also star rated.

The guide to shopping describes the different types of establishments and what services they offer and what you can buy (including recommended picnic food). There are useful phrases and lists of groceries with simple phonetics to help you ask for them.

The recipes, using typical Spanish ingredients like peppers and chillies, garlic and sherry, will appeal to cooks of all abilities.

A short section highlights the types of food and dishes eaten on high days and holidays and advises on what is seasonally available.

Trying to understand the menu can sometimes be a nightmare. The **Eating Out** section gives advice and phrases to use in a variety of establishments, as well as hints on how to order drinks. There are also tips on catering for babies and children, special diets and coping with a tight budget.

To round off there are more phrases, with a pronunciation guide, and conversion tables to help with shopping and cooking.

INTRODUCTION

Spain has developed, almost separate from
Europe, in its own unique way. This is because
it is cut off on land by the high Pyrenees and
stands on a peninsula with oceans on two sides.
For almost 1,000 years after its conquest by the
Arabs in AD711, Spain's cultural links were with
North Africa. During this time the
preoccupation of Spaniards was to oust the
conqueror, and as the Arab Moors were driven
out, they were replaced by a number of
separate kingdoms. Though the country united
under the 'Catholic Kings' Isabella and
Ferdinand in 1474, provinces like the Basque
country and Catalunya have continued to assert
their individuality. This regionalism is reflected
in the cooking.

Another important factor was the discovery of
America in 1492 and the formation of Spain's
vast empire. This imperial past is still
remembered. In Spain 'America' means the
continent of Latin America. From the new lands
came chocolate, long a Spanish monopoly, as
well as tomatoes, peppers (at first just a
flavouring for tomato), potatoes, maize, sugar
cane and numerous varieties of beans. The
Spanish adopted them all and invented recipes
to make use of them long before they became
familiar elsewhere.

*Farmhouse near
Torremolinos in
southern Spain.
The use of fresh
local produce is
the hallmark of
Spanish cooking*

INTRODUCTION

The fishermen of Spain keep up the supply of ever popular seafood

Poor communications hampered relations within Europe, though links with Italy go back to the Romans. The second recipe book in Spanish, printed in the 1600s, was largely a translation from Italian. During the 19th century it was Italian chefs who raised the reputation of the new Spanish restaurants.

Spain never learned the sophisticated kitchen techniques practised in France, though the Napoleonic army which invaded Spain found much of interest to take back to France. The French contribution came much later, when *nouvelle cuisine* inspired the Basques to their own *nueva cocina vasca*. The Spanish cooks adopted the aspects of that new style that suited them – the emphasis on freshness and local ingredients. The results were good: better versions of the local dishes that they had always made, produced with a new confidence.

The food of provincial Spain makes a healthy diet. The middle classes may eat too much meat, but local food is based on vegetables and rice, fish, salad and beans.

Spanish wine has also immeasurably improved – and so has its reputation. Scarcely 30 years ago the wines of Rioja were sold (unnamed) 'from a vineyard 320km/200 miles south of Bordeaux'. Now Rioja is appreciated for its velvety treasures, while *fino* sherry is recognised as one of the world's great wines.

THE REGIONS OF SPAIN

Spain is a country of fierce regional pride. Wherever you are, just here in this particular corner of Spain, you will be told, grow the best beans, or asparagus, or peppers in the world. The cooking is well-matched to the ingredients and recipes are regional – or develop their regional variations.

Andalucía

In Andalucía you will find the essence of all that is Spain – flamenco dancing, bull-fighting and brown *sierras* (mountains) – often topped by the black bull silhouette that splendidly advertises Veterano brandy. It is a huge area of the south, cut off from central Spain by the Sierra Morena.

The Arabs marked the landscape by planting olives and oranges. They created a cuisine based on spices like cumin and saffron, and ingredients such as olive oil and nuts, all ground with mortar and pestle. Their chilled soups, such as the white garlic and almond AJO BLANCO, made with local muscat grapes, and GAZPACHO (now made with tomato and pepper) are welcome in the summer heat. It is here that *tapas* were invented, to sustain evenings that end in a mere five hours' sleep. One of the best *tapa* is sliced SERRANO, raw ham cured above the winter snow line at places like Trevélez. The Costa del Sol is celebrated for its fried fish. The fried fish take-away was invented here in the great seaport of Cádiz, and the city is now known for its PESCAÍTO FRITO (mixed fried fish), while every beach-bar on the coast offers squid rings in batter. Málaga is famous for deep-fried little CHANQUETES (gobies, or other tiny fish) and fresh anchovies, with their tails stuck together then fried in the shape of a fan. The area is also known for skate with paprika, grilled swordfish steaks and fish soups, like CALDILLO DE PERRO. A fish stew worth searching out is URTA A LA ROTEÑA.

From Jerez de la Frontera, where your sample of FINO is hurled through the air into a glass, come sherry dishes such as kidneys in sherry or stewed bull's tail (RABO DE TORO AL JEREZANA). In Seville 'duck with orange' was invented (PATO A LA SEVILLANA).

Tomatoes and peppers were first introduced here 400 years ago and appear in many local dishes, like PIPIRRANA (pepper salad) and flamenco eggs, the colourful gypsy mixture of different vegetables with eggs. Another 'traveller's dish' is OLLA GITANA, a stew which can include any vegetable or fruit. Desserts in the south are eaten in small spoonfuls as they are incredibly sweet, like quince paste and TOCINO DE CIELO, a jelly of syrup and egg yolks. The best, however, are the little Arab cakes, such as the almond ALFAJORES of Medina Sidonia and the crumbly POLVORONES in Antequera. Try also the YEMAS, which are rich little egg yolk candies, made by nuns.

Levante

Named for 'where the east wind blows', the Levante takes in

THE REGIONS OF SPAIN

most of the east coast, from Cartagena northwards. It includes the orange-growing areas of Alicante and Valencia – and a good many sunshine beaches, like Benidorm. This is the land that the legendary medieval hero El Cid won back from the Moors.

But the Arabs introduced rice, and Valencia is the home of the famous PAELLA – originally cooked outdoors – and other rice and fish dishes, including ARROZ A BANDA and el CALDERO. Rice is also partnered with beans in the black and white dish MOROS Y CRISTIANOS (Moors and Christians).

The market gardens here produce wonderful vegetables, while the big Albufera lake yields both ducks and eels. ANGUILA AL ALI-PEBRE is a spicy way of serving the latter.

The most famous fish dish of this area is DORADA A LA SAL, bass baked in salt, but the grey mullet is also good, as is an unusual brown mussel *(datil de mar)*. Other specialities include cured fish, like MOJAMA and GIRABOIX, which is a salted cod stew. The coast is also a centre for pickled capers – delicious with fried fish.

As well as oranges, figs and muscat grapes are plentiful, while Elx-Elche has the world's largest date grove. A milky summer drink to try is HORCHATA, made from tiger nuts, while the whole of Spain buys almond TURRÓN from Jijona at Christmas.

Catalunya and the Balearics
Catalunya (also known as Cataluña or Catalonia) embraces both the Pyrenees (Pirineos) and the Costa Brava. Barcelona restaurants have been famous for over 100 years and the city is now one of Europe's best places to eat. ZARZUELA and SUQUET, two

Traditional farming on Menorca

ebullient fish stews that burst with shellfish, are made here, as is the wonderful crazy mixture LANGOSTA CON POLLO (lobster with chicken), while LLAGOSTA A LA CATALANA is likely to be lobster with chocolate! PARRILLADA is a grilled dish which includes fish and shellfish (or fish with meat), often with chilli and nut ROMESCO sauce. Salted cod is so popular here that it is sold ready-soaked, for dishes like XATÓ, the Tarragona salad. Or try the pasta and shellfish mix called FIDEUÀ. Duck with figs, or gosling with pears, are characteristic poultry and fruit combinations, while duck with olives and rabbit with snails are other celebrated pairings. Vich is known for charcuterie, and excellent black and white BUTIFARRA sausages are made here.

Grills are a speciality including COSTELLADA, lamb chops with local sausage, eaten with the pungent ALIOLI (garlic sauce). Indeed, barbecues produce some of the best food, like ESCALIVADA (baked whole vegetables), barbecued spring onions eaten at the feast called *calçotada*, and grilled snails, eaten at the CARGOLADA feast. In winter, warming vegetable stews such as ESCUDELLA DE PAGÈS are a welcome feast, and wild mushrooms, particularly ROVELLON, are a passion. Well-prepared spinach, ESPINACAS A LA CATALANA, is eaten with the flat bread called *coca*. And you will find that in Catalunya all meals start with a tomato bread called PA AMB TOMÀQUET.

The English occupied Menorca in the Balearic Isles (Islas Baleares) in the 18th century – and left gin and gravy (*grevi*) behind as proof! The French found MAHONESA (mayonnaise) there in the 1770s, and took the recipe home. But the Balearics are best known for very solid, heavy dishes made with lots of bread, like SOPA MALLORQUINA, and vegetable stews like TUMBET. Stuffed squid, fried poultry in sauce (ESCALDUMS), and SOBRASADA (a soft red sausage) are other local dishes. The pizza-like COCAS MALLORQUINAS are traditionally baked in outdoor ovens, and pies, large and small, are island favourites. There is a local cheese, too – MAHÓN.

Catalunya gave the world a favourite dessert, *crème brûlée* (CREMA CATALANA), but try also the almond cream (MENJAR BLANCO), and simple curds with honey (MEL I MATÓ). PANELLETS and ROSCOS in Barcelona and BUNYOLS on the coast are among the little cakes to look out for. Catalunya is also home to some of Spain's best white wine, as well as champagne-style fizz.

New Castile and La Mancha

High on Spain's central plateau, this is Don Quixote and windmill country, centred on the nation's capital. The temperatures here are extreme – bitter winter cold and parching summer heat. Madrid is home to all styles of cooking, with many good authentic regional restaurants. It also has a robust nightlife. Its most famous meat dishes are COCIDO MADRILEÑO, where several meats are simmered together for hours, and a beloved nursery dish of stewed tripe (CALLOS) found in all the *tapas* bars. You will also find good roast meat, baked bream (*besugo al horno*) and a local salted cod dish, SOLDADITOS DE PAVÍA. To the south, near the exquisite former royal summer palace at Aranjuez, strawberries and asparagus grow.

Castile (Castilla) is the country's bread basket, growing excellent wheat, pure and very white; from it a distinctive round bread is made – and also wheat soup. The bread is the ideal accompaniment for the local tomato stew (PISTO MANCHEGO). Beans and lentils are local crops, while Zamora is chick-pea country. The plains also grow Spain's 'yellow gold', saffron, the world's most expensive spice. And it is said that TORTILLA, the national egg dish, has its origins in Castile, invented by a peasant for a hungry king.

Castile is the partridge capital of Spain. The bird is used for *perdiz estofada* (braised partridge) and jellied ESCABECHE, besides mixed game pâtés like GAZPACHO MANCHEGO and MORTERUELO.

The plains are famous for sheep, and for the country's most distinguished cheese, MANCHEGO. Try it breadcrumbed and fried as QUESO FRITO.

Madrid *fiestas* are well known for their sweet pastries, like the cream-filled BUÑUELOS and the sugared bread TORRIJA, made for children. Toledo, the old capital, is famous for MAZAPÁN, made into little *figuras* for Christmas. LECHE MERINGUADA is a sweet summer drink, while the wine-soaked cakes, BIZCOCHOS BORRACHOS, can be eaten in any season.

Old Castile and Rioja

Cut off from Madrid to the south by the Guadarrama mountains (Sierra de Guadarrama), Old Castile runs north to the Cordillera Cantábrica. Three great medieval cities are sited here – Avila, Salamanca and Segovia.

This is the centre of the *zona asados*, for here the best roasts are prepared in the old beehive Arab ovens, called *hornos de asar*, characteristic of Segovia, Valladolid and Burgos. The secret is that the meat is not cooked quickly, as you might expect for young animals, but roasted gently and slowly for succulence. At Avila and Segovia, COCHINILLO (suckling pig) is an institution, though LECHAZO (milk-fed lamb) is sometimes rated even higher.

Although the area boasts many of Spain's best red wine vineyards, the Rioja also grows wonderful peppers. Indeed dishes with 'a la riojana' in their name are likely to include them, for example PATATAS A LA RIOJANA. Lots of beans are grown and eaten dried, as well as green, and fresh beans (POCHAS) are eaten with quail or sausage. Baked aubergines and white asparagus, sold in cans throughout Spain, are other specialities. Castilian garlic soup is well known, especially at Avila. The monastery there also makes the sugary yellow cakes called YEMAS.

Aragón and Navarra

Aragón and Navarra embrace the northern end of the

Pyrenees and their foothills, a country dotted with monasteries, for pilgrims poured through Roncesvalles and other valleys on the pilgrim route to Santiago de Compostela, one of Europe's holiest Catholic shrines. With them they brought French-style dishes like MENESTRA DE VERDURAS (a vegetable stew). One simple traveller's dish is salted cod in BACALAO AL AJOARRIERO.

Mountains mean good lamb, grilled as chops, roast young as TERNASCO, or stewed as COCHIFRITO. Here 'mountain asparagus' means lambs' tails, lopped in spring! Real asparagus grows at Tudela and is used in TORTILLAS. The foothills slope down to the banks of the warm Ebro river, where red peppers are grown, in particular the slim and very spicy PIMIENTOS DE PIQUILLO. At Lodosa these peppers are protected by an *appellation contrôlée*, and eaten stuffed with meat or salted cod. The region is even better known for red pepper stews called *chilindrones*.

Fast streams in the mountains breed trout, and *truchas a la Navarra* are fried in ham fat and served stuffed or wrapped in ham. The opening of the hunting season is celebrated with POCHAS CON CODORNICES, the first quails, eaten with fresh kidney beans. Partridges are often deliciously served with chocolate sauce. Rabbit is stewed with garlic, wine and rosemary, while fried sausages with eggs are popular, too. The black Aragón MORCILLA

Shepherd in the Pyrenees

sausage includes both rice and pine nuts, while the CHORIZO of Pamplona-Irunea is simply the best *tapa* sausage.

Hidden in the Pyrenees, the Val d'Arran was once cut off from the rest of Spain for six months of the year by bad weather until Franco built a tunnel to it. Now skiing has made the area fashionable, and good chefs have rushed to open *bordas*, 'barn restaurants', where the food is earthy but invariably good. Local specialities include pigeon with raisins (PICHÓN CON PASAS Y PIÑONES). Aragón has its own cheese in RONCAL. It is also known for junket (CUAJADA), sold in brown pots resembling flower pots and eaten with honey. The foothills bear

THE REGIONS OF SPAIN

orchards of apple, cherry and peach, and peaches in red wine are a delicious local delicacy.

There is a Basque tradition of cod fishing in the Atlantic

Basque country and Cantabrican coast

In their tiny corner of Spain, snuggled next to the Bay of Biscay (Golfo de Vizcaya) and the mountains that lead to France, the Basques are self-styled 'gourmets', with a restaurant for every thousand inhabitants! Here men-only associations, called *cofradías*, cook and eat gourmet meals – the women wash up! Anywhere in Spain, a Basque name on a restaurant (an unpronounceable title with TX in it) means it is likely to be first-rate.

The Basques have traditionally looked outward, beyond their own territory, for influence and inspiration. Firstly there is a French Basque region, too – and dishes like the soft, un-Spanish omelette PIPERRADA prove it. Then Basques are the rovers, the Atlantic fishermen bringing home great catches of cod. Their shipboard stews such as MARMITAKO, and other dishes made with BONITO tuna are well known. Among dozens of salted cod recipes, BACALAO A LA VIZCAINA is the most famous.

The area is also celebrated for the most delicate fish dishes, including MERLUZA EN SALSA VERDE (hake in a green parsley and pea sauce), exquisite fried sole, and BACALAO PIL-PIL, requiring an especially light chef's touch.

The name *donastia* (Basque for San Sebastián), is given to many local dishes, so expect to be a little confused! Other fishy luxuries are TXANGURRO (stuffed crab) and CHIPIRONES EN SU TINTA, best here when squid are line-caught, not in nets where they lose the ink that makes the black sauce of the dish.

Eating ANGULAS (elvers) in winter started in the Basque eating clubs, and the fashion spread. Another rarity is KOKOTXAS, pieces of hake cut from the throat, best made into fritters.

The Cantabrican coast, where many Spanish families take their holidays, is known for its small fish restaurants. Dishes include clams or baby sardines in sauces, and fresh local trout and salmon. RABA is an unusual squid dish with the squid first coated in breadcrumbs, then fried.

The green Basque countryside grows fresh peas, green beans and artichokes in season, made into casseroles like MENESTRA. It is also known for broad beans, eaten fresh. Dried beans (such as kidney beans) are made into soups like *baba-txikis* or stewed with sausage, like the bean stew of Tolosa. Guernica is famous for *choricero* peppers, used to make local sausages and roast peppers with chops. The Basques make a good leek and potato soup with salted cod (PURRUSALDA), and they are also keen mushroom-hunters.

Local meat is good, with plentiful roasts, enormous steaks and good lamb and game dishes, like CODORNICES EN HOJAS (quails in vine leaves). The Cantabrican coast is known for chicken with rice (CAMPURRIANO). This is also dairy country, however, and the local Basque cheese is smokey IDIAZÁBAL, while a mild blue PASIEGO is made at Pas. Desserts to tempt include custard horns (CAÑUTILLOS) and INTXAURSALSA, an unusual walnut cream.

Galicia and Asturias

The extreme west is Spain's Celtic fringe – a misty, green, apple-growing country. The landscape is studded with little *horreos*, sheds built on stilts for storing maize and cheeses. In the far west, the vines are grown up on pergolas, unusual for Spain. Powerful drinks like QUEIMADA bolster you against the harsh Atlantic winds!

In the western bays huge, tender orange mussels grow beneath structures that resemble Chinese junks, and indeed the whole area is famous for its seafood. Dishes to try include LANGOSTA, the excellent lobster, while Santiago de Compostela has its own lobsters (*santiaguiños*) – and of course the pilgrims' scallop dish, VIEIRAS DE SANTIAGO. A strange and costly shellfish is the tubular black barnacle, PERCEBES. At festival time big octopuses are displayed on all the bars, to be served as spicy PULPO AL FERIA. RAPE (monkfish, called *pixin* here) is cooked in cider. Varieties of fish are placed in layers to make a delicious CALDERETA, while small cuttlefish and sardines are made into pies. Freshwater fish include salmon.

This is tripe and sausage country, home of the black MORCILLA of León, which goes into Asturias' famous bean dish, FABADA. Lentils and chestnuts are also much used. Galicia's best known stew is LACÓN CON GRELOS, a ham knuckle cooked with young turnip tops.

Butter and lard are much used in cooking, and a number of meats are cooked in milk. Duck with turnips is claimed as a Galician recipe, and chickens taste excellent when roasted in

THE REGIONS OF SPAIN

pork fat or cooked with beans or rice. There are also many pigeon and partridge dishes. In the wilderness of Asturias, game such as chamoix and capercaillie is hunted. Local cuisine is simple fare – chestnut soup and CACHELADA, a stew with fine potatoes and CHORIZO, are good examples. Huge heads of cabbages, some a metre (3 feet) high, will catch your eye as you drive through Galicia and these go into broths like CALDO GALLEGO. Many lettuces are grown in this part of Spain, while locals claim watercress was first eaten here. The tiny green peppers from Padrón are sold all over Spain usually to be deep-fried whole.

EMPANADAS are giant pies made with peppers and tomatoes, plus fish or pork, and further inland they may be topped with bread dough, rather than pastry. Rye bread is a local speciality, while cornmeal is used for bread (BORONA) sometimes stuffed with meat (*prenada*).

Spain's most famous creamy blue cheese, CABRALES, comes from Asturias, and distinctive fresh REQUESONES (cottage cheeses) are made. Favourite cheeses include Galician smoked SAN SIMÓN, which looks like an amber pear, and the soft, breast-shaped TETILLA.

Asturias is known for the best milk in Spain and not surprisingly you can enjoy many milk puddings: rice travelled north as ARROZ CON LECHE. Look out too for the varieties of sweet pancake, like the Galician liqueur-flavoured FILLOAS. About 250 varieties of apples are grown locally, together with plums and pears. Desserts include apple tarts, pears in red wine with cinnamon (invented here), and superb sugary MARRONS GLACÉS.

Extremadura

The name means 'extreme and hard' and the west of the region, bordering Portugal, has some of the most beautiful mountain scenery in this mountainous country. Chestnuts, cork oaks and the evergreen holm oak, whose acorns feed the black pigs, grow in abundance.

The most famous ham in Spain is produced here, at Jabugo, where the snows of the *sierras* give it its popular name, SERRANO – 'mountain' ham. The best hams are those from the wild *pata negra* pig. Superb hams are also made at Montánchez. As you might expect, there are also excellent CHORIZOS and MORCILLAS. In a restaurant an *entremes de carne*, a sliced selection, is one way to try the local cured meat. Sausages also go into the local TORTILLA, while PRINGADAS are bread strips fried in bacon fat. Garlicky croûtons, called MIGAS, are made to eat with savoury dishes, and also served as a sweet with a chocolate sauce!

Local delicacies include frogs, small eels, partridges and turkeys, while the monastery at Alcántara is famous for its luxury pheasant dish (FAISÁN AL MODO DE ALCÁNTARA). Mountain lamb is the meat in the stew, COCHIFRITO; use is also made of tongues, liver, and there is a local kidney dish, RIÑONADA. Jellied ESCABECHE and freshwater tench are also relished.

A-Z GUIDE TO SPANISH FOODS

A

Abadejo
Pollack. A less flavourful fish than hake (MERLUZA) but cooked the same.

Abichón
Silverside or sand smelt. A good fish when tiny and deep-fried like whitebait.

◆◆ Acedias fritas
Fried baby soles. A popular *tapa* in the southwest.

Aceite de girasol
Sunflower oil.

Aceite de oliva
Olive oil. Usually 'pure' (which is a mixture of virgin and refined oil) and labelled with its acidity – 0.8° is perfect.

Aceitunas
Olives. *Aceitunas aliñadas* are marinated olives, that is, cocktail olives.

◆◆ Aceitunas rellenas con anchoas
Green olives with anchovy stuffing. Newest and nicest of the cocktail olives.

Acelga
Swiss chard or spinach beet. A vegetable with gleaming white stems and bitter dark leaves, much loved in the south. You will find it *fritas* and *guisadas* (fried and stewed); in MENESTRA, a general vegetable stew; in rice and bean soup and as a TORTA, which may have a little sugar in it, too.

◆◆ Acelgas con pasas y pinones
Chard fried with plump raisins and crisp pine nuts, sometimes called *a la malaqueña*. A similar dish, *a la catalana*, includes anchovies as well.

Achicoria
Chicory.

Aderezada
With dressing. Many canned, cooked vegetables are sold like this.

Aderezo de mesa
Condiments.

Adobo
Marinated before cooking. *Lomo adobado* is marinated pork loin for roasting or frying.

Agua de azahar
Orange flower water. For flavouring desserts.

Aguacate
Avocado. *Con gambas* means it is stuffed with prawns.

Aguja
Gar or needlefish. A couple of

Olive trees in the Sierra Nevada

feet (60cm) long and with a nose like a knitting needle. The backbone is green, but do not let this bother you. Good poached.

Agujas, en
On skewers.

Ahumado
Smoked. You can guess *salmón ahumado*.

◆ **Ajada, allada**
Garlic, paprika and oil beaten to make a sauce. Used to dress hot fish and vegetables.

Ajedrea
Savory (the herb).

◆◆ **Ajetes**
A springtime speciality of young garlic shoots, pulled from the centre of the bulb. Wonderful with scrambled eggs, they are also pickled as *brotes de ajo*.

Ajiaceite, al
In garlic oil. The simplest of Spanish sauces used, for example, with snails.

Ajilla, en
In a garlic sauce, usually a pan sauce. Often thickened after frying with garlic puréed with bread.

Garlic: a love of this pungent bulb is an advantage in Spain

Ajo, al
The dish has whole garlic cloves in it. Do not be too frightened of these; garlic becomes quite mild after long cooking. It is raw garlic that makes the smell!

Ajo arriero
'In the mule-drivers' style', that is, dressed with garlic, paprika and parsley. These chaps were the forerunners of truckers, moving goods across the country. The places they stayed at *en route* were too poor to cook anything fancy, and these dishes are simple, made with eggs, or vegetables like cauliflower, or salted cod.

◆◆◆ **Ajo blanco con uvas de Málaga**
A most delicious chilled almond cream soup (white GAZPACHO), flavoured with garlic and garnished with muscat grapes.

◆◆ **Ajo colorado**
Creamy salted cod pounded with bread and garlic and coloured red with paprika. It is

a red version of the French
brandade, and Lent food.

◆ Ajo de la mano, el
Literally 'garlic in the hand', this
is potatoes cooked with chillies,
then dressed with pounded
garlic, cumin, oil and vinegar.

◆ Ajoaceite
Castilian for ALIOLI, usually a
smooth, dense garlic sauce, with
egg yolks and even mashed
potato or breadcrumbs.

Ajonjolí
Sesame seeds. Popular in little
festival cakes.

Ajopollo, en
'In the sort of garlic sauce
chicken is served in', with
almonds; see PEPITORIA.

◆◆ Alajú
A rich, flat medieval cake.
Dense, very dark and made
with honey and whole toasted
almonds, like Italian *panforte*.

Albacora
The long-finned tuna with white
flesh. It is less dense than ATÚN,
and considered the best tuna.

Albahaca
Basil.

Albardado
Barded (wrapped in fat or fat
meat, eg ham), or battered or
crumb-coated.

Albaricoque
Apricot. Dried fruit are called
OREJONES.

◆◆ Albóndigas en salsa
Meatballs in sauce, usually
tomato. A popular *tapa*, they are
often made of veal and pork.
The same word is used for fish
cakes.

◆◆ Albufera, salsa
A cream and red pepper sauce,
sometimes with ground almonds
in it. Good with fish.

Alcachofas
The big flower buds of globe

artichokes. In the middle of
each one is a bristly choke
(which has to be removed)
above the edible soft base.
Prepared bases are often
served as salads. *Aliñadas*
means 'marinated' and *con
mayonesa* is with mayonnaise.
They are also included in many
salads and hot rice mixtures.

◆ Alcachofas al vinagreta
Artichokes served boiled and
warm, or cold, with vinaigrette.
To eat, the leaves are pulled off,
each base dipped into the
sauce, then just the soft flesh
pulled off with the teeth.

◆◆ Alcachofas rellanas
Artichokes stuffed in the
middle, often *con atún* (tuna).

**◆◆ Alcachofas salteadas con
jamón**
Sautéed artichoke bases with
ham. The bases are also braised
in Montilla, or served with
potatoes, in a saffron broth (see
recipe page 102).

Alcaparras
Capers. These grow wild and
the pickled flower buds are
particularly good with fried fish.

Alcaravea
Caraway seed.

◆◆◆ Alfajores
An individually-wrapped,
Christmas almond and honey
candy, invented by the Arabs.
The ones made in Medina
Sidonia are sensational.

Aliño
A simple vinaigrette, or an oil
and salt dressing. *Aliñado*
means marinated, or dressed,
vegetables or fish.

◆◆◆ Alioli, all-i-oli
This is one of the great Spanish
sauces, to be tried at least once
in a lifetime. Take a vote that
either everybody in your party

eats it or nobody, because it does make the breath smell quite powerfully, as puréed raw garlic is the main ingredient. This is whisked to an emulsion with oil and sometimes egg yolks too. One of the best sauces for prawns barbecued in the shell and grilled fish or chops, it is also stirred into fish soup. In Catalunya, *aliolis* of puréed fruit and garlic are served with roast lamb.

Almadrote
A sauce of mashed garlic and hard cheese, usually cooked with aubergine.

◆◆ **Almejas**
Clams. Raw or cooked in wine or spicy tomato sauce, clams are popular seaside fare, though

Almonds, found in many dishes

fiddly to eat when small. In *almejas con arroz*, clams and onions flavour rice.

◆◆◆ **Almejas a la marinera**
Clams fisherman's style, with white wine, a little oil and parsley.

Almendras, tostadas
Toasted almonds. They are popular with drinks. Everything from soup (*sopa*) to trout (*trucha*) can be *almendrada*, made from, or cooked with almonds. See PEPITORIA for almond sauce with chicken. *Almendras garrapiñadas* are almonds in toasted sugar.

Almíbar, en
In syrup. The Arabs invented syrup, and probably peaches in syrup too.

Alpargatas
The name means *espadrilles* and these 'shoe-shapes' can be sweet biscuits in the north. They can also be meat patties, coated in whisked egg white before frying, which gives them the appearance of rope-soled shoes.

Alubias
Dried kidney beans of lots of different colours. Tolosa is famous for black beans (*alubias negras*). Beans *a la vizcaina* are typical: stewed with a little TOCINO (pork fat), onion, garlic and parsley.

Amanida
The Catalan word for salad. Probably an arranged salad including fish and meat, if it is *a la catalana*.

Amargo
Bitter.

◆ **Amargos, amarguillos**
Little, dry Arab marzipan cakes.

◆◆ **Amarilla, en**
A yellow sauce, made from

onions and saffron, thickened with egg yolks.

◆◆ Ametlles
Catalan for almonds; also delicious toasted almonds, coated in praline or chocolate.

Anacardos
Cashew nuts.

Anchoas
Canned anchovies. *En aceite* (in oil).

◆ Andaluz, salsa
Andalucían sauce. It is a fair bet that it will include garlic, tomatoes, peppers and pumpkin. *A la andaluza* is with red peppers and tomato.

Añejo
Aged (of cheese etc)

Angelote
Angelfish, and a small shark, with a tail like RAPE, but less good to eat.

Anguila
Freshwater eel. *Angula* is elver – baby eel. These look like silver spaghetti and are an expensive luxury in winter.

◆◆ Anguila al ali-pebre
Valencian speciality of eels in an oil and paprika sauce.

◆◆◆ Angulas a la bibaina or en cazuela
A Basque speciality of baby eels tossed in chilli oil and served from an earthenware casserole with wooden forks.

Anis
Aniseed. One of the great flavours of Spain, much used for biscuits by adding one of the many anis-flavoured liquors.

Anona
Custard apple.

Apio
Celery; *apio ensalada*, celery salad.

Araña
Weever fish. For soup.

Arándano
Bilberry.

Arencas
Salted and pressed sardines.

Arenque
Herrings, usually fried simply.

Arete
Red gurnard. A fish with firm white flesh, of good flavour and not-too-difficult bones. As it is slightly dry, it is best cooked in sauce.

◆ Arrope
A grape juice or honey syrup. Used for sweetening wine and for simmering dried fruit.

◆◆ Arròs amb crosta in Catalan, **arroz con costra** in Castilian.
A famous PAELLA, with meat-balls, pieces of poultry and pork, cooked in the oven. The egg crust is broken when the dish is served.

Arròs amb fesol i naps
A soupy Valencian rice dish, with beans, turnips and pieces of pigs' ears, trotters, etc.

Arròs brut
Soup dish with meat and game.

Arròs de peix
More a soup than a rice dish, with fish.

◆◆◆ Arròs negre
Black rice. It is a speciality of the Costa Brava. Cuttlefish colour the rice with their ink.

Arroz
Rice.

◆◆◆ Arroz a banda
A famous two-course Valencian fish and rice dish. The rice, flavoured with saffron and fish stock, is served first. The fish, which were cooked in the stock, then follow, often with ALIOLI.

Arroz caldoso
Rice soup, often made with fish.

A–Z FOOD GUIDE

> **Rice: A Basic Ingredient for a Variety of Simple Dishes**
>
> Rice is used to make many simple dishes in Spain, like *ensalada* (rice salad). In the north, rice dishes are called *arroz*, when they would be called PAELLA in Valencia, for example *arroz con almejas* (with clams) or *arroz marinera* (fisherman's style). *Arroz a la catalana* will have BUTIFARRA sausage and peppers; *arroz a la vasca* has chicken giblets; *a la cubana* comes with fried bananas and eggs; *huerta* with 'market garden' vegetables; *arroz a la alicantina* includes fish, artichokes and green peppers; and *a la zamorana* has chopped pig's cheek and trotters.

Mallorcan street market

◆◆ Arroz con leche

A cold rice pudding, flavoured with lemon and cinnamon. Popular in the northwest. *Requemado* has a grilled sugar top.

◆ Arroz empedrat

'Dappled rice' because it combines rice with broad beans and tomatoes. Nicknamed 'factory rice' as it was devised for the nougat workers at Jijona.

Arroz en perdiú

A Lent dish, the name means 'rice with partridge', but the 'bird' is only a whole garlic bulb.

Asado

From the oven, so roasted. *Asadillo* is roast, skinned peppers reheated in little dishes with garlic.

◆◆ Atascaburras

On the east coast, this is a purée of salted cod with potato and pine nuts, similar to the French *brandade*. The name is also given to a heavily garlicked rabbit stew – see CONEJO.

◆◆ Atún
Blue-fin tuna. It is a treat fresh, grilled in big (bloody) steaks or baked. It may be cooked, marinated and served cold (*escabeche*), or made into small hot pies (*empanadillas*). See also ALBACORA, called *atún blanco*.

Avellana
Hazelnuts. Popular in sauces and pâtisserie.

Avena
Oats.

Aves
Birds.

Azafrán
Saffron. This Arab spice is much included in rice and stews in the north as well as south. It is always expensive, but beware of imitations if you are buying it to cook! Buy the stamens.

Azahar
Orange blossom.

Azúcar
Sugar. *Azúcar moreno* is brown sugar – *azucarillos* is candy floss.

B

◆◆◆ Bacalao
Cod. Not a Mediterranean fish, though it may be fresh on the Atlantic coast. It is hugely popular salted and dried, and much eaten in Lent. It does not taste salty after soaking. Leave it 24 hours in a bowl of cold water, under a dribbling tap. It soon makes still water smelly, so the water must be changed regularly. Then remove all skin and bones and cook as fresh. In Catalunya it is called *bacallá*

and is cooked *en samfaina* (in tomato sauce). It is good fried in fingers (*soldatitos*), makes tasty BUÑUELOS (deep-fried potato puffs), and wonderful salads, like ESQUEIXADA.

◆◆◆ Bacalao a la vizcaina
The most famous hot dish made with salted cod. The sauce includes the piquant peppers of the region and sweet ÑORA chillies. Well-made, it is wonderful, but it can be pretty grim: fish, pools of oil and sparse, too-spicy pepper. Outside the Basque country, the sauce often includes tomatoes too. *Bacalao a la riojana* is very similar, with peppers and paprika.

Bacalao al ajo arriero
Salted cod mashed with garlic and parsley, 'the mule driver's way'. It is always a pale dish, but can contain scrambled egg.

◆ Bacalao pil-pil
A Basque dish of hot salted cod. It is gently rocked in the casserole until the gelatine from the fish makes an emulsion, and so a very light white sauce, just from cooking oil and garlic.

◆◆ Bajoques farcides
Red peppers stuffed with rice and meat or BACALAO.

Bandarillo
A cocktail stick with bits of cheese or ham; named after the barbed stick used in the bullfight.

Barbacoa, de
Barbecued.

Barbo
Barbel (freshwater fish).

Barquillo
A thin rolled wafer, made on a mould. In Madrid these are stuffed.

◆◆ Bartolillos
Triangles filled with custard, then deep-fried – a speciality of Madrid.

Batata
Sweet (white) potato.

◆◆ Becadas
Woodcock. They are roasted or pot-roasted. May be stuffed with their own gizzards, or these may be pounded for the sauce.

Beicón, bacon
Leanish pink breakfast bacon.

Berberechos
Cockles. Less sweet than clams, they are made into sauces or served in soup or rice.

Berenjenas
Aubergines. Introduced by the Arabs. *Al horno* is baked, *fritas* is fried and they are also moulded (*molde*).

◆ Berenjenas a la catalana
Fried aubergines cooked in tomato sauce.

◆◆ Berenjenas rellenas
Stuffed aubergines with minced beef as well as garlic, breadcrumbs and chopped egg, sometimes fish.

Berros
Watercress.

Berza
Green cabbage. Often included in soups or MENESTRA. *Bertón* is a stuffed cabbage.

◆ Berza andaluza
A mixture of chick-peas or dried beans with cabbage, ACELGA or green beans, flavoured with salt pork or other bits of the pig.

◆◆◆ Besugo
Red bream, with a black spot on the shoulder. A favourite fish in Spain, it is good grilled or baked with lemon and oil (*a la madrileño*) or in white wine (*al vino blanco*).

◆◆◆ Besugo a la donastiarra
Red bream grilled over a charcoal fire.

◆◆◆ Besugo asado con piriñaca
Baked bream with chopped red peppers.

Bien me sabe
Means 'I know it does me good', given as an excuse to eat something delicious. There is a fish dish and also a very rich Andalucían dessert of ground almonds and cinnamon with this name.

Biftek, bistek
Beef steak. Ask for it *poco hecho* for underdone, *regular* or *muy hecho*.

◆◆ Biftek salteado al jerez
Fried steak with a little sherry used to make a sauce with the cooking juices.

Bizcocho
Sponge cake. The word covers all types, even sponge finger biscuits. It may be *de almendras* (with almonds) or *a la crema* (with cream).

◆◆ Bizcochos borrachos
'Drunken' cakes soaked in wine or syrup, then sugared.

◆ Bocadillo
A sandwich of a crusty roll, sprinkled inside with olive oil, and often filled with ham and cheese.

◆ Bocadillos de monja
This 'nun's mouthful', is a small cake made of almonds, sugar and eggs.

Bocadito
A 'mouthful' – often found on biscuit packets.

Bogovante
The true lobster.

◆ Bola
Béchamel-based croquette, served deep-fried.

Boleto
Cep mushroom.
◆◆ Bolets amb pernil
A simple dish of ceps and ham.
Bollo
A common word for a bread
roll, also a sweet bun; (see also
SUIZOS). *Bollo de panizo* is a
cornmeal scone, eaten with
vegetables. *Bollo preñado* –
'pregnant roll' – has meats
cooked inside.
Bomba
Meatball, or potato shape,
served with chilli sauce.
Bombón
A chocolate.
Boniato
The orange-fleshed sweet
potato: America's 'yam'. It is
made into sweet puddings with
cinnamon; cooked then dipped
into syrup; and puréed.
◆◆◆ Bonito
Means 'pretty', and this light,
white-fleshed tuna, with a dark
striped back, is highly prized. It
is good grilled or baked, and
makes MARMITAKO.
◆ Boquerones
Fresh anchovies. They taste
quite different from canned
ones (ANCHOAS). The best come
from L'Escala. They are
marinated and served pickled
as an *ensalada* or *en vinagreta*.
◆◆ Boquerones a la malagueña
Several fresh anchovies are
stuck together at the tail to form
a fan, then are floured and fried.
Borona
Cornmeal bread.
◆◆ Borra, la, borreta
A salted cod and potato soup
with spinach, flavoured with
sweet chilli.
Borracho
Grey gurnard (fish), with firm
but dry white flesh. Best baked.

Lobster fisherman off Menorca

◆◆ Borrachos, borrachuelos
These 'drunkards' are
doughnuts or cakes soaked in
wine or syrup.
◆◆ Botifarra amb mongetes
Catalan BUTIFARRA sausage
stewed with dried white beans.
◆◆ Bou estofat, buey estofado
Catalan beef stew, with sweet
RANCIO wine, BUTIFARRA, potatoes
and possibly wild mushrooms.
Bover
A large edible snail; see
CARACOLES.
◆◆ Brasa, a la
Grilled on a grid over the
embers (*brasas*). Meat *a la
brasa de sarmiento* is cooked
over vine prunings. The best!
Brasear
To braise.
◆◆ Brazo de gitano
'Gypsy's arm'. A well-known
cake, like a Swiss roll, but
brown, longer and thinner. It is

A–Z FOOD GUIDE

rolled up with cream or chocolate custard. There is also a version with potato.

Breca
Small bream. Good grilled or baked; see DENTÓN.

Brécol, bróculi
Broccoli. *Broquil* in Catalunya, where it is very popular.

◆ Brevas
Small yeast doughnuts, deep-fried with a custard filling. *Breva* is also the black early-ripening fig.

Brocheta
A skewer or spit.

Brotes
Sprouts, bean sprouts or, in the Basque country, the spring side shoots of cabbage.

Buey
Ox, so stewing beef.

Buey
The big-clawed crab.

Bullit
The Mallorcan version of COCIDO.

◆◆ Buñuelos
Fried puffs, often served as *tapas*. The lightest ones are made of choux pastry, with additions – like *buñuelos de queso* (cheese puffs). *Buñuelos de bacalao* are often based on mashed potato – a good way to try out salted cod. Others are coated, crisp fried morsels: like *sesos*, made with brains, which are very creamy inside, or *apio*, from celery. Sweet fritters are made from apricot (*albaricoque*) and puffs are soaked in syrup (*al aguamiel*).

◆◆ Buñuelos de viento
Choux puffs 'as light as the wind' says the name. San Isidro is celebrated in Madrid with cream-filled ones.

Bunyettes
Yeast doughnuts.

◆◆ Bunyols
Warm, sugared, deep-fried doughnuts. Popular on the Costa Brava, sometimes cream-filled.

◆◆ Burgos, queso de
A fresh ewes' milk cheese, a bit like a drum-shaped mozzarella.

Búsano
Whelk.

◆◆◆ Butifarra
A big banger, the white sausage made from pork or veal, of Catalunya. It is frequently cooked with beans (*con habas*). There are also black *butifarrones*.

C

Caballa
Common mackerel. An oily fish, it is best baked (*al horno*) – good *a la gaditana* – or stewed with potatoes. See also ESTORNINO.

Cabello de ángel
'Angel's hair' comes from a squash (CIDRA), with very stringy flesh. It is stewed or made into a popular jam, which is much used in shop pastries.

Cabeza de ternera
A 'head-cheese' (ie a seasoned loaf) of jellied veal. *Cabeza de cerdo* is brawn.

◆◆ Cabra
Goat. Both *cabrito asado* (young roast kid) and *caldereta de cabra* (stewed kid) are good.

Cabracho
The ugly, spiny, copper-red scorpion fish. A great soup-stew ingredient.

◆◆◆ Cabrales
A creamy blue cheese. A

Goats provide both milk and meat

cheese to challenge Roquefort, and, like it, stored in limestone caves, where it acquires its blue veining. It is generally made of cows' milk and shaped like a small drum without pressing. It is finally wrapped in maple leaves.

Cabrillo
Comber (fish). Used for soup, though the tail is worth eating.

Cacahuetes
Peanuts.

◆◆ **Cachelada**
A Galician stew using the new potatoes called *cachelos* with CHORIZO.

◆ **Cailón**
Porbeagle shark. Good to eat, especially the barbecued steaks.

Calabacines
Courgettes. They are baked (*al horno*), stuffed (*rellenos*) and made into fritters (*fritos*).

Calabaza guisada
Stewed pumpkin, often included in vegetable sauces in the south. *Calabazote* is a pumpkin, potato and bean stew.

◆◆ **Calamares**
Squid. Batter-fried squid rings

(*a la romana*), are a common *tapa*. Small ones are cooked in their own ink, *en su tinta*, in the north – see CHIPIRONES. In the south, small *calamaritos* are often served in a tomato, pepper, paprika and fish sauce.

◆◆ **Calamares rellenos**
Stuffed squid. The stuffing may be pork and almonds (*a la catalana*), or grated cheese with pine nuts, breadcrumbs and parsley (*a la levantina*), while in Mallorca raisins are added.

◆◆◆ **Calçots**
A Catalan word for spring onions as thick as a finger, which are a speciality of Valls in Tarragona. At *la calçotada*, a spring feast, they are eaten direct from the barbecue with ROMESCO sauce.

◆◆◆ **Caldereta de cordero**
Stewed lamb, particularly good when thickened by the lamb's liver. In Extremadura it includes red peppers, MIGAS and the local sausages as well; in Seville, a good slug of sherry. There are also quail (*codornices*) and rabbit (*conejo*) versions.

◆◆◆ Caldereta de pescados
On the north coast this is a layered fish casserole, often with potatoes, and there are versions with shellfish and even lobster (*langosta*). These may be served liquid first, as soup, then the fish.

Caldero
A cooking pot or small cauldron. *Caldereta*, *caldeirada* are the stews that come out of it. *El caldero* on the south coast is a soupy rice and fish dish.

◆◆ Caldillo de perro
Little 'dog soup'. It is made of fresh small hake, flavoured with bitter orange juice and is a speciality of Puerto de Santa María on Cádiz harbour.

◆◆ Caldo gallego
A hearty Galician soup, containing white beans, turnip tops and a ham bone.

Caliente
Hot.

Pavement restaurant in Madrid

Callos
Stewed tripe. Popular in *tapas* bars across Spain.

◆◆ Callos a la catalana
Stewed tripe dish which may include pine nuts and rich RANCIO wine.

◆◆ Callos a la madrileña
Typical stewed tripe dish. Highly spiced with ham and CHORIZO. Chick-peas are often included, as they are in Galicia and Andalucía.

◆◆ Camarones
Tiny shrimps, white in Cádiz.

◆ Camerano, queso de
A soft, fresh goats' milk cheese from Rioja.

Campurriano
'From the country' (*campo*). *Pollo campurriano* in Santander is a rice dish with chicken, bacon, peppers, shallots and wine.

Caña de dulce
Sugar cane; also a puff pastry finger with custard filling.

Caña de vaca
Marrow bone.

Cañadilla, cañailla
Sea snail, like a whelk with knobs on. Eaten cold as a starter. This is the *murex* from which the Roman Imperial purple dye came. It will not stain your mouth though, as the dye only develops exposed to the sun.

Canela, con
With cinnamon. This spice goes into many savoury dishes and replaces vanilla as the main flavouring of custard, ices and chocolate desserts. In Spain it is usually included in biscuits and cakes.

Canelones
Cannelloni, stuffed and covered in sauce. In Spain they are sold

as roll-them-yourself squares of pasta.

◆◆ Canelones a la barcelonesa
Cannelloni stuffed with ham and chicken livers (*foie gras* if you are lucky), in a tomato and sherry sauce. They are then topped with béchamel sauce and grilled.

Cangrejo (de mar)
The large-clawed crab.

◆◆ Cangrejos de rio
Freshwater crayfish. Messy to eat, but very good, cooked with tomato, brandy and chilli.

◆ Cantabria, queso de
A flattish round cheese, semi-hard and made from cows' cream in a celebrated cheese area in the north.

Cañutillos de crema
Pastry custard horns.

Cap roig
Scorpion fish. Can be baked if large, but is mostly used for soup; see ESCORPENA.

◆◆ Capirotada, la
Meat hidden by a 'hood' of almond sauce. The dish may be made from rabbit, chicken or other small birds and even meatballs.

Capitón
Type of grey mullet; see LISA.

Caqui
Kaki or persimmon, a winter tree fruit. Very acid unless it is soft, yellow and like an over-ripe tomato.

◆ Carabineros
Enormous, showy scarlet prawns with purplish heads, named for their military colouring. They are not as good value for money as LANGOSTINOS, being a bit bland, so their flavour is boosted with brandy. They are often made into soup.

Caracoles
Snails. A popular country food, often just served with vinegar. *Sin trabajo* means out of their shells – 'no work'!

◆◆ Carajitos
Hazelnut macaroons. The best being *de profesor*.

Carbonero
The black-backed coalfish, coley or saithe. Cooked like MERLUZA.

Cardamomo
Cardamom.

Cardo
Cardoon, related to the globe artichoke, though the stalks are blanched in plastic, rather like celery. These are eaten in white sauce, often with ham, or braised.

◆◆◆ Cargolada, la
A snail feast in Catalunya; *cargol* is a snail.

Cari
Curry.

Carn d'olla
See ESCUDELLA.

Carne
Meat; means beef without further description. *Carne de vaca* (cow) is the main Spanish beef, not of particular quality. *Carne de buey* (ox) also makes good beef stews.

◆◆ Carne de buey en estofado
A stew, usually with root vegetables. *A la catalana*, it may have BUTIFARRA (white sausage) and chocolate in it, and *con peras y castañas* is with pears, thickened with chestnuts.

Carne de lidia
Bull's meat. Dark red, tough and strong in flavour – not sold in ordinary butchers.

Carne picada
Minced meat.

A–Z FOOD GUIDE

Carnero
Mutton. Excellent *estofado* (braised) or *con ajo* (with garlic) for it has more flavour than young lamb.

◆◆ **Carnero verde**
Mutton dish from Tenerife. Braised with chopped parsley, mint and lettuce heart, with lemon juice and spices.

Carquinyolis
Almond biscuit, made hard by slicing the loaf and rebaking the slices. Its crumbs are used for thickening meat sauces.

Carrillada
Pig's cheek. Stewed in sherry in the south.

Cártamo
Safflower. The false saffron, bright yellow, but without the incomparable taste.

◆◆ **Casadielles**
Little sweet puff-pastry turnovers, filled with ground walnuts, then baked or fried.

Castañas
Chestnuts. They are made into a simple cream soup, flavoured with cinnamon, and are also cooked *con leche*, in milk, as a pudding with sugar.

Caza
The 'hunt' and so game.

Cazón
The smooth-hound, one of the best edible sharks, because it feeds on shellfish. Its steaks are white, firm and somewhat dry.

◆◆ **Cazón en adobo**
Is marinated in paprika and vinegar, then battered and deep-fried. Good in Cádiz.

Cazuela
Spain's commonest brown cooking pot. It gives its name to any stew that comes out of it. Little *cazuelitas* are much used for cooking individual portions

of fish – with plenty of sauce – and for eggs and mushrooms.

Cebollo
Onion. *Cebollone* is the Castilian for CALÇOT. *Cebolletas* are spring onions and *cebollinos*, chives. *Encebollada* means in onion sauce.

◆◆ **Cecina**
Dried beef eaten raw like ham, (what Americans call 'jerky'), *ceniza* in Catalunya. There is a tuna version.

Centeno
Rye. A black bread made in Galicia.

◆◆◆ **Centollo**
Spider crab. There is only meat for one person on each crab, for its claws are small and empty. The flesh is stronger and sweeter than that of clawed crabs, so often mixed with hake, brandy, parsley, garlic and lemon and stuffed back into the shell. This may be grilled.

Cerdo
Pork, the common meat.

Cerezas
Cherries.

◆ **Cervera, queso de**
A fresh ewes' milk cheese, made in Valencia.

Ch
Note the Spanish alphabet has 29 letters, not 26. CH is considered a separate letter and follows C in Spanish lists.

Chacina
Minced pork or sausage filling. *Chacinería* are pork products – charcuterie.

Chalotas
Shallots.

◆ **Champiñones**
Cultivated mushrooms. Often served *al ajillo* (with garlic) like wild ones. They are good *rellenos*, stuffed with sausage or

pork and crumbs, or fried with ham.

◆◆ Chanfaina
A stew eaten on the day of pig killing, the *matanza*. It contains the lungs, lights, head, etc of the pig with the liver. However, do not confuse this with dishes such as *pollo en chanfaina*, which is chicken in SAMFAINA sauce.

◆◆◆ Changurro, txangurro
The Basque term for CENTOLLO, a popular *tapa* potted.

◆◆ Chanquetes
The over-fished gobies, slim silver fish, nicknamed 'sea spaghetti' and a Málaga speciality. This is now a term for any tiny fried fish, battered and deep-fried.

Cherna
Wreckfish or stone bass, a grouper. Cooked like MERO.

Chicharones
The crackling made from pork skin, left when fat is rendered. This is sold as a snack and is sometimes included in bread.

Chicharro
Coarse horse mackerel or scad. Best grilled.

◆◆◆ Chipirones
Tiny squid. Good when stuffed with their own tentacles and served in a sauce of their own ink (*en su tinta*).

Chirimoyas
Custard apples. Eat them with a spoon, spitting out the big seeds. They are very smooth and creamy when ripe.

◆◆ Choco
A small cuttlefish. Stewed *con habas* (with beans).

Chocolate
Chocolate is not good in Spain, except in the Basque country. The bars are poor quality; only the breakfast drink is good.

◆ Chocolate, marquesa de
Chocolate mousse is flavoured with cinnamon or orange.

◆◆ Chopa
Red or black bream. Good to eat; see DENTÓN. Excellent *a la sidra* (in cider).

Chopitos
Small cuttlefish; see SEPIA.

◆◆◆ Chorizo
The scarlet sausage, flavoured with the *choricero* (chilli) which

Chorizo *and other delicacies*

A–Z FOOD GUIDE

is sweet but not very hot. There are two types of sausage. The fatter one is the equivalent of salami, eaten sliced on bread. The other is stewed with beans and soups, or fried, and comes hot or mild.

◆◆◆ Choto
Baby kid; see CABRA.

Chufa
Tiger nut. This is the tuber of a type of sedge. Made into the chilled drink HORCHATA, sometimes iced.

Chuletas de cerdo
Pork chops. Usually dusted with paprika and fried or grilled, then served with a little lemon juice.

Chuletas de cordero
Lamb chops. A luxury.

◆◆ Chuletas de cordero a la navarra
Lamb chops in a sauce of ham, onion and tomato.

◆◆◆ Chuletas de cordero al sarmiento
Tiny (and expensive) lamb chops, grilled over vine prunings.

◆◆ Chuletas de ternera
Veal chops, big and juicy. Best *a la riojana* (with roast red peppers).

Chuletón
An enormous wing rib beef chop. Beef is best in the north of Spain.

◆ Chumbo
Cactus fruit or prickly pear. Very refreshing. The trick is to peel them with knife and fork, avoiding spines.

◆◆ Churros
Breakfast fritters. These ubiquitous fritters are sold in every market, the dough being piped in circles into the hot fat before your eyes. The fritter rings may then be threaded with a reed for carrying them,

and sugared. Good with breakfast chocolate or coffee.

◆◆ Churrusco
Means 'scorched', and so barbecued; often spare ribs.

Cidra
A big squash with stringy flesh. It is boiled in sugar to make a favourite jam; see CABELLO DE ÁNGEL.

Ciervo
Deer. The meat is tough, so best stewed with herbs.

◆◆◆ Cigalas
Not to be missed, these are what the Italians call *scampi* and the English, Dublin Bay prawns. There is some meat in the claws, but most in the tail. Unlike other prawns, they are pink when raw. Eat them boiled or grilled, with coarse salt.

Cilantro, culantro
Coriander. Fresh leaves are used in the Canary Islands.

Ciruelas
Plums and greengages. *Ciruelas en aguardiente* are bottled in *eau-de-vie*.

Ciruelas pasas
Prunes. Very good soaked in anis.

Clavo
Cloves (literally nails).

◆◆ Coca mallorquina
Next cousin to the Italian pizza, with tomatoes and onions and often sausage on top – less often cheese. Sweet ones include currants or candied fruit.

◆◆◆ Cochifrito a la navarra
Milk-fed lamb stewed almost without vegetables, just lemon juice, garlic and paprika or saffron.

◆◆◆ Cochinillo asado
Suckling pig, roasted when so young and tender it can be carved with the edge of a plate.

Langostas, langostinos *and* cigalas: *succulent lobsters and prawns*

Cocido
'Cooked' in Spain really means simmered. *Cocido de col* is simply simmered cabbage.

◆◆◆ Cocido madrileño
Spain's national meat dish of salt pork, beef and stewing hen, simmered in a pot with chick-peas. A second pot contains cabbage and CHORIZO. Sometimes PELOTAS (meat dumplings) are simmered too. The meal is served in two or more courses. First the broth (*caldo*) with rice in it as soup, often the cabbage and sliced sausage second, and then the sliced meats and chick-peas (sometimes with tomato sauce or pickles) last.

Every region in Spain has its own *cocido*, often with more vegetables. For example the Basques include red beans, while in the south they tend to be sweeter, with pumpkin or sweet potatoes – and every region includes its own local sausages; see ESCUDELLA.

Coco
Coconut. *Cocos* or *cocados* are little coconut cakes.

Cóctel
Cocktail, as in *de mariscos* (seafood cocktail).

Codornices
Wild quail. These are large and plump like French ones, not tiny farmed birds. See also POCHAS CON CODORNICES, ZURRÓN.

◆◆ Codornices al ajillo
Quail, roast or pot roast with wine or garlic, often stuffed with their own gizzards.

◆◆ Codornices en hojas de parra
Quail wrapped in vine leaves.

Cogollo
Means a 'core' or 'heart'. Often quartered lettuce hearts, but also artichoke bases and *cogollo de palmito* (palm heart).

Col blanca
White cabbage. Served AJIACEITE, or *rellena* (stuffed).

Cola
Tail. *Cola de vaca* is oxtail; see
RABO DE TORO.

Coliflor
Cauliflower.

◆ Coliflor frita
Marinated cauliflower,
crumbed, or just egged, then
fried, is good.

Collejas
Lambs' lettuce or corn salad.

◆ Colmenilla
Morel mushroom.

Comino
Cumin. Introduced by the
Arabs, it has become a basic
barbecue spice.

Compota
Cooked dried fruit.

◆◆◆ Concha fina
The big Venus shell clam, with a
mahogany-coloured shell. It is
eaten raw, with chilled FINO.
Inside it is a glory of scarlet and
orange, hence the name 'fine
shell'.

Concha peregrina
Scallop. Their shells were the
badge of Santiago pilgrims; see
VIEIRAS.

Seafood tapas *in Barcelona*

◆◆ Conejo
Rabbit; *del monte*, if it is wild.
This popular food is commonly
stewed (*guisado*) with onions,
herbs and wine, or with cider in
the north. A gravy with
chocolate is common.
ATASCABURRA has plenty of garlic,
CAPIROTADA has an almond
sauce. Pies and cold jellied
rabbit *al vinagreta*, or EN
SALMOREJO, are also popular.

◆◆ Conejo con caracoles
A combination of snails and
rabbit, both 'free food'. The
snails feed on rosemary and so
flavour the meat.

Congrio
Conger eel. Good with *salsa
verde*; see MERLUZA.

◆◆◆ Consomé al jerez
Correctly *caldo* (broth) laced
with sherry and the founder of a
great tradition of clear soups.

Coques, coquetes
Flat breads; see COCA.

◆ Coquinas
Wedge shell clams. Eaten raw,
or like ALMEJAS.

Corazón
Heart. Best stewed and often
included in a lamb stew.

Cordero
Lamb. A luxury but it is rarely eked out with vegetables when it is stewed.

◆◆◆ Cordero al chilindrón
An Aragón speciality of lamb stewed with red peppers.

◆◆◆ Cordero al pastor
Stewed lamb, seasoned with a little garlic and saffron and a sauce thickened with its own liver.

◆◆◆ Cordero asado
Roast lamb. At its best from a baker's oven. Watch for *horno* outside restaurants in Old Castile. The very best are *cordero lechal* or *mamón* (suckling lamb).

◆◆ Cordero asado a la manchego
Lamb roasted in an earthenware dish with garlic and onions.

Corvina
Meagre (fish). Good to eat fried, or cooked like LUBINA.

Corzo
Roe deer.

◆◆ Costellada
Lamb chops grilled over an open fire with BUTIFARRA.

◆◆ Costillas a la parrilla
Spare ribs grilled or baked (*al horno*). Excellent with ALIOLI.

Costra
Means 'crust'. So with cheese (*costrada manchego*) it becomes toasted cheese.

Costrada
Can be a pastry slice (or a *millefeuilles*) with custard and fruit, or a slice of cake with a candied top.

◆◆ Costrada navarra
A layered soup of CHORIZO or bread and vegetables, soaked in broth then baked with eggs on top to make a crust. This is a common way of presenting thick soups.

Crema
A purée soup; can be sweet.

◆◆◆ Crema catalana
One of the great cream desserts. The custard is strongly flavoured with cinnamon and lemon zest, then fiercely grilled with a minute amount of sugar on top. The result is a net of caramel and a slight taste of the grill. This *crème brûlée* is served very cold.

◆◆ Crema de San José
A chilled egg custard; see NATILLAS.

Cremadina
A custard filling – French *crème pâtissière*.

Cremat
Catalan for 'burned'. It is used for their wonderful pudding and for flamed coffee. *Pescado al cremat* means fish in 'burnt garlic' sauce: really cooked to a rich golden brown.

Criadillas
Testicles, made into fritters.

Criadillas de la tierra
Truffles; see TRUFA.

◆◆ Croquetas
Deep-fried croquettes. A popular *tapa*, they are made of minced meat, bound with egg, or based on béchamel sauce, egged, crumbed and fried. These may also be made with BACALAO, shrimps (*quisquillas*) or spinach (*espinacas*).

◆◆ Cru de peix
Literally 'raw fish', a quick-cooked fish stew with saffron and paprika.

Crudo
Raw. *Para comer crudo* to eat raw.

◆◆ Cuajada con miel
Junket (very like yoghurt). Sold

in little straight-sided earthenware pots and eaten with honey, and also made into a cheesecake. *Cuajo* is rennet, that curdles the milk.

Culantro, cilantro
Coriander.

D

Dátiles
Palm dates – a super-sweet fresh fruit.

Delicias
A little *tapa* biscuit or spongecake. For *delicias de hojaldre*, see PALMERAS.

◆◆◆ Dentón
Dentex (fish), a bream with pinkish tints. It makes very good eating, especially grilled or baked with onion (*al horno*). Little and lesser breams tend to end up in soup.

Despojos
Offal.

Dorada
The best and most expensive of the breams, called a gilt-head because of its golden eyebrow.

◆◆◆ Dorada a la sal
Dorada baked completely encrusted with salt, then hammered open at the table. A party dish, and a Murcian speciality.

Dulce
Means 'sweet', and hence is used for sweets. Stiff cold fruit pastes, such as *dulce de membrillo* (quince) are common, and also desserts like *dulce malagueño*, semolina with egg yolks, sugar, raisins and quince.

◆ Duquesa
A pie shaped like a little English

pork pie, it may contain fish or vegetables. *Duquesitas* are smaller and sweet.

E

Eglefino
Haddock. Found smoked but rarely fresh.

Emborrachada
'Drunken', so marinated or in wine sauce.

Embutido
A fresh sausage; literally 'stuffed'. Home-made, it is *a la casera*.

◆ Empanada de lomo
Pork loin and pepper pie, called *de raxó* in Galicia. Pies are also made of fish, such as the skinny, yellow-fleshed *xouba* and *de vieieras* (scallop pie); others are made of BACALAO.

◆◆ Empanada de Pascua
Easter pie of young lamb.

◆◆ Empanadillos
Popular small savoury pies. Tuna and tomato are good – and rather spicy if they are *murciana* – or they may be pork or ham with spinach. The dough is sold ready-cut in packets. The name includes sweet doughnuts, which may contain jam
– CIDRA.

Empanados/. . . das
Means 'breaded' and then fried, for example cutlets.

Emparador
Swordfish; see PEZ ESPADA.

Emparedado
Sandwiched, literally 'enfolded'. The sandwich is soaked in milk, then fried and served hot (*caliente*).

◆◆ Empedrada, la
This 'speckled' dish is a Catalan
salted cod salad with broad
beans.
Encargo, por
Made to order.
Endibia
Chicory (in white heads).
Enebro
Juniper berry.
Eneldo
Dill.
◆◆ Ensaimada
A delicious sweet yeast roll in a
spiral, served for breakfast in
Mallorca. Larger ones, the size
of pizzas, may be topped with
slices of SOBRASADA (red pork
sausages).
◆ Ensalada
Salad. The best-known salad is
crisp lettuce, onion rings and
olives, perhaps with tomato
slices. However, *ensalada mixta*
is likely to be an elaborate
mixture of vegetables in a
larger restaurant. Other
possibilities are *lechuga*
(lettuce), *tomate* (tomato), *de
habas* (cooked beans), perhaps
dressed with mint, and seasonal
salad (*del tiempo*). They are
accompanied by oil and
vinegar, to dress yourself.
◆◆ Ensalada de San Isidro
This salad named after the saint
of Madrid contains lettuce with
marinated ATÚN (tuna).
◆◆ Ensaladilla
Means 'little' or Russian salad, a
mixture of cooked, diced potato
with peas, carrots and artichoke
bases in mayonnaise.
◆◆ Entrecot a la pimienta
Steak with peppercorns, *not*
chopped vegetable peppers.
Entremés variados
Assorted appetizers. *De carne*
is a selection of sliced meats.

Farming the red soil of Ibiza

◆◆ Erizos de mar
Hedgehog sea urchins. They
are broken and eaten with a
spoon like a boiled egg,
combined with scrambled egg,
or used for a creamy sauce.
Escabeche
Pickled by cooking in wine and
vinegar. Fish, meat and
vegetables like aubergines are
all cooked this way, then left
until cold. *Escabechado* means
pickled.
◆◆◆ Escabeche de perdices
Partridges cooked in wine and
a lot of vinegar, then chilled till
the liquid jellies. Rabbit, *conejo
en escabeche*, is also good.
◆◆ Escaldums
Chicken or turkey pieces are
panfried, then finished in an
onion and tomato sauce,
thickened with almonds and
SOBRASADA sausage.
◆◆◆ Escalivada
A delicious salad of cold, baked
vegetables, like aubergines and

peppers, dressed with virgin oil and sometimes anchovies. The name means 'barbecued'. Tomatoes may be included too. The vegetables may be puréed and served chilled.

Escaloña
Shallot.

Escarola
Endive.

Escorpena, escorpión
Scorpion fish. Mostly used for fish soups, but the flesh (under the venomous spines) is good if served filleted.

◆◆◆ Escudella i carn d'olla
The Catalan COCIDO of boiled meat. It includes ham, chicken, cubed veal, BUTIFARRA and dried and fresh vegetables. The broth is served first, then the meats and vegetables. *Escudella de pagès*, is 'country style', with carrots, potatoes and cabbage.

Espada, pez
Swordfish. *Filetes* are good grilled. See also PEZ ESPADA.

Espadin
A sprat; whitebait if they are very small.

Espaldilla
Shoulder of beef. Good pot-roast.

◆◆ Espárragos con dos salsas
White canned asparagus with vinaigrette plus mayonnaise or a sauce of chopped tomato.

◆◆◆ Espárragos trigueros or **amargueros**
Wild (bitter) asparagus, which once 'grew among the wheat'. A spring speciality, best with scrambled eggs (REVUELTOS), it is also sautéed or baked with crumbs.

Especias
Spices. Spanish spices date from Moorish times. Cinnamon (*canela*), surprises by appearing in many savoury dishes. *Comino* (cumin) was liked by the Moors and is a main ingredient in the spice mix *pinchitos morunos*. In specialist shops, mixtures are sold for tripe, snails, fish and for *adobos de carne* – meat marinades. *Colorante* is also sold to dye PAELLA yellow.

Espeto, al
Cooked on a spit.

Espinacas
Spinach. It makes soup with GARBANZOS (chick-peas) and is stewed in a mixed MENESTRA.

◆◆ Espinacas a la catalana
Spinach tossed in butter with anchovy, pine nuts and raisins.

◆◆◆ Esqueixada
A Catalan starter salad of slivers of red pepper, tomato and raw salted cod.

Estofado
This does NOT mean stuffed, but braised. *Estofado de buey* is beef stew. It will include roots like carrots and turnips in the northwest, and potatoes in the south. *Estofado a la catalana* may contain chocolate.

Estornino
Spanish mackerel, with pinkish oily flesh. Of good quality, so some people prefer it to CABALLA (common mackerel).

Estragón
Tarragon.

F

Faba, fave
A large buttery-textured dried bean. Normally stewed with garlic and paprika.

◆◆◆ Fabada asturiana
A famous slow-cooked bean dish in Asturias, with ham and

salt pork and made spicy with saffron, MORCILLAS and CHORIZOS.

◆◆ Fabes a la granja
Spain's top white beans: *a la granja* indicates a superior dish.

Faisán
Pheasant.

◆◆ Faisán a las uvas
Pot-roast pheasant in port, served with grapes.

◆◆◆ Faisán al modo de Alcántara
Europe's most celebrated game dish: pheasant stuffed with its own liver and truffles. It is marinated, roasted and served with truffle and port sauce. The recipe was discovered in a Spanish monastery by a looting Napoleonic army and promoted by French chef Escoffier.

Falda rellena
Stuffed flank.

Faramallas
Sweet fritter in Galicia.

Farro
This vegetable soup takes its name from pearl barley, but sometimes it contains vermicelli instead.

Faves, fabes
Beans. Used for FABADA in Asturias, but also eaten in the south in vegetable stews like *faves al tombet*; see TUMBET.

Fesol
Type of dried bean.

Fiambre
Cold pressed meat (though a *fiambre de bonito* is made from tuna). *Fiambre de ternera* is veal pâté.

Fideos
Vermicelli. Now sold in a variety of thicknesses. They are popular in soups.

◆◆◆ Fideuà a la mariscos
A wonderful shellfish PAELLA – but made with FIDEOS, not rice.

Filete
A fillet – of beef or fish.

◆◆ Filloas
Large crêpes, cooked on a griddle like the Breton ones, jam- or custard-filled.

◆◆ Flamenquines
Originally rolled-up ham and cheese, deep fried as a *tapa*. Sophisticated versions may include pork or be enclosed in béchamel and a crumb coating before frying.

◆◆◆ Flan de huevos
Moulded caramel custard and Spain's national sweet, excellent if *a la casa* (home made). *Flan de naranja* is made from orange juice.

◆◆ Flaó, flaón
Sweet cheesecake, often flavoured with anis. Tiny ones are pastries with curd cheese.

Barcelona restaurant menu

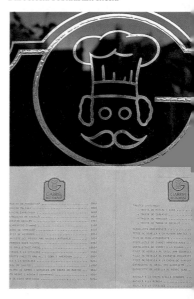

◆◆ Flores
Sweet fritters, made in the west.
They may be 'flower-shaped'
(*de manchego*) and are
sprinkled with honey or sugar.

Frambuesas
Raspberries.

Francesa, a la
In the French style, that is, with
a white sauce.

Frejol
Type of dried bean.

Fresas
Strawberries. Usually without
cream. Delicious *con anis* or
with OLOROSO sherry.

Fricadelas
Meat patties.

◆ Fricandó
Small pieces of beef or veal,
fried, then finished in a sauce.

Frijoles
Dried beans. In the Canary
Islands, black beans and rice
are *frijoles con arroz*.

Frio
Cold.

Frito
Fried, so *fritos* are fritters. A
fried dish, *frite de cordero*, is
excellent made with young

lamb. *Fritillos* (little fritters) may
be sweet.

◆◆◆ Fritura de pescado
A fry-up of mixed fish; *fritura a
la gaditina* or *malagueña* are
deliciously crisp.

◆ Frixuelos
Sweet pancakes served with
honey.

Fruta
Fruit. A list of fruits is given on
page 96. Some less familiar fruit
worth trying, all of them
half-wild in Spain, are figs
(*higos*), pomegranates
(*granadas*) and prickly pears
(*chumbos*).

◆ Frutas de Aragón
Crystallised fruits which are
then chocolate-coated.

Fuerte
Strong, ie highly spiced,
possibly with added vinegar.
'Something stronger' (*más
fuerte*) means alcoholic if
applied to drinks. *Fuerte* means
bitter or unripe, if applied to
fruit.

*Tantalising display of fruit in
Barcelona's La Boquería market*

G

Gachas
Gruel. A survivor from medieval times, made with wheat or other flours (like GOFIO). It can be milky and sweet (with aniseed and lemon) or flavoured with garlic and ham. In some places it is so thick that it sets when cold (like porridge) and slabs are then fried. There is a garlic and potato version in the south.

◆ Galets, sopa de
Galets are small pasta, and this pleasant soup also contains small meatballs. It is flavoured with fresh celery leaves.

Galletas
Any crisp biscuits.

Gallina
Hen, suggesting a well-stewed chicken dish.

Gallineta
Norway haddock (also called bluemouth and red fish) and related to rascasse. Famous for soups. Its firm flesh is good cooked like bream; see DENTÓN.

Gallo
A cock.

◆ Gallo
A popular flatfish and so the equivalent of our small plaice. It is best plain fried with plenty of lemon juice squeezed over.

Galludo
Dogfish or small shark. Good to eat; see CAZÓN.

Gamba
One of the best prawns, sold raw in Spain. Needs 2–3 minutes in boiling water.

◆◆◆ Gambas con gabardinas
'Prawns in mackintoshes', battered then deep-fried until crisp; a popular *tapa*.

◆◆◆ Gambas pil-pil
Prawns sizzling in plenty of oil and garlic, made very hot with chilli. Mop the juice up with your bread (see recipe pages 107–8). The dish has no relation to the BACALAO of the same name. In the south, it is sometimes called *piri-piri* after a similar Portuguese dish.

Ganso
Goose, see also OCA.

Garbanzos
Chick-peas, the potatoes of Spain. They need soaking, then 1–1½ hours' simmering. The equivalent of crisps are *salteados*, nutty and ready-sautéed as a snack, or toasted (TORRADOS). *En remojo* in a market, means 'soaked' for cooking. *Refritos* means boiled then fried in a new dish.

◆ Garbanzos con espinacas
A pleasant stew of chick-peas, spinach and garlic, perhaps with tomato and peppers.

◆◆◆ Garbanzos y chorizos
The perfect combination of nutty chick-peas with spicy sausage to flavour them.

◆ Garbure navarro
A Spanish version of a French soup, with a mixture of vegetables and salt pork, and probably CHORIZO.

Garrapiñadas
See ALMENDRAS.

◆◆ Gatavask
Also called *gâteau basque* and *pastel vasco*, this is a heavy sweet-pastry tart, with set custard, jam or fruit inside. Excellent for picnics.

◆◆◆ Gazpacho
The famed chilled soup is made from puréed bread and garlic, with raw peppers, tomato and cucumber, made creamy with

oil and vinegar; this is labelled *sevillana, andaluz* or *rojo*. The Madrid version includes mayonnaise. In winter it is served hot (*caliente*).

♦♦♦ Gazpacho blanco
A creamy white version of GAZPACHO, based on garlic, vinegar and almonds *con uvas* (with muscat grapes).

♦♦ Gazpacho manchego
A rich mixed game pâté. The liquid is thickened with breadcrumbs like *gazpacho* soup, which explains the name.

♦♦ Gazpachuelo
A creamy soup, served just warm, based on mayonnaise, sometimes thinned with fish soup. It may contain potatoes and their cooking water. The connection with GAZPACHO is the vinegar in it.

Gelats
Catalan for ices. Try the *gelat d'amentilla* (almond sorbet) in Mallorca.

♦♦ Giraboix
A salted cod stew with vegetables, including green beans and cabbage, as well as potatoes, served with ALIOLI. The highly-seasoned broth can be served as soup first.

Girasol
Sunflower. Unripe black seeds are crushed to make a bland cooking oil. The white seeds are eaten as a snack.

Glorias
A little sweet pastry (sometimes a meringue) with an almond or sweet potato filling.

Gofio
Toasted cornmeal. In the Canary Isles, this is made into balls as a substitute for bread.

Golosina
A sweet titbit.

♦ Granada
Pomegranate, not the city. The fruit is hard outside and full of red jewelled seeds inside. Soak it in hot water to make it easier to peel. Swallow or spit out the tiny seed enclosed in each capsule of juice, as you please. *Granadina* may be a syrup of the juice.

Granadina
Grenadine, the yellow passion fruit. Or see above.

♦ Granizado
A grainy fruit sorbet or, sometimes, iced drink: the Spanish version of the Italian *granita*. The Catalan is *granissat*.

Gratinado
Au gratin.

♦ Greixera
A Mallorcan casserole. There are meat ones, and layered vegetable and egg ones, like *greixera d'ous*. One is like a quiche filling without pastry. Desserts are made too, all in the shallow round-bottomed casserole, the *greixonera*.

♦♦♦ Greixera a llagosta
Lobster gratin, with a spinach and egg sauce.

♦ Greixonera de brossat
A cheesecake in Mallorca, made with REQUESÓN. Less commonly, a baked bread-and-milk pudding.

Grelos
The spring leaves and flower buds of turnip tops, stewed; see LACÓN CON GRELOS.

Grosellas
Red or black currants.

Guinda
Cocktail or glacé cherry.

Guindilla
The one hot chilli in the Spanish kitchen, found in cold Galicia. The name means 'cherry-red'.

They are used for cooking, and sold dried as *rama*, and pickled in jars.

◆◆ Guirlache
A hard toffee containing toasted almonds and aniseeds.

Guisado
Stewed. This may be a stew of vegetables alone, eg *guiso de espárragos amagueros* (stew of wild asparagus).

◆ Guisantes
Peas. Often stewed with ham *a la española*, or tomatoes, and included in MENESTRA and many veal dishes.

◆ Guiso de trigo
Historic soup with wheat grains, and probably chick peas and turnips too.

H

Habas
Fresh or dried broad beans. *A la catalana* is beans cooked with TOCINO (pork fat) and BUTIFARRA. *Ensalada* is a bean salad, which includes mint.

◆◆◆ Habas con jamón
Fresh broad beans combined with fried ham, parsley and hard-boiled eggs. It is also called *habas españolas, rondeña* and *a la granadina*.

Habichuelas
Green summer beans.

Hamburguesa
Hamburgers. In Spain, they are made of minced pork, and pork and beef mixtures, as well as all beef.

Helado
Ice-cream is sold in the usual European flavours: *de vainilla, de chocolate* and *de limón*, all of which you can guess.

Stop off for a refreshing ice

Strawberry is *de fresas*. The most popular ice-cream in Spain, which accompanies fruit salad, etc, is *canela* (cinnamon) which also makes an unusual sorbet. Other unusual Spanish ices are *moscatel* (muscat grapes) and *turrón* (nougat). A *copa* is a sundae, while a *tartahelada* is an ice-cream cake with a sponge layer. An ice-cream cone is *un cucurucho*.

◆ Helado quemado
Ice-cream in a pot, topped with grilled sugar.

Hervido
Poached, from *hervir* (to bubble or boil).

Hierba buena
The 'good herb' is mint. It dates back to the Arabs.

Hierba Luisa
Lemon verbena.
Higadillos, higiditos
Chicken livers. *Salteados* are
sautéed, and they are much
used with rice and eggs.
◆◆ Higado de ternera
Calf's liver. *Con cebolla* is with
fried onion and often ham.
Higado guisado is stewed
lamb's liver with onions and
potatoes.
Higos
Figs.
Hinojo
Fennel. Wild in Spain, it is
added to fish and used for
salad.
Hojaldre
Layered like 'leaves', and so
puff pastry. The Spanish

probably invented it, though
their version is a bit heavy.
Usually it is sweet, for example
cream slices, but *hojaldre de
salmón* is salmon pie.
Hojas de parra
Vine leaves. Served stuffed with
minced meat and bread, or
wrapped round birds such as
quail.
◆◆ Hongos
The wild mushrooms that grow
on tree stumps. Excellent with
crêpes or eggs. *A la andaluza*
they are cooked with sherry or
Málaga wine.
◆◆ Horchata
Tiger nut drink, sometimes an
ice-cream; see CHUFA.
◆ Hornazo
A 'baked' Easter cake,

Egg Dishes
As well as the basic cooking
methods, eggs are treated
as a separate course in

Huevos a la flamenca

Spain. *Huevos a la riojana* are
baked with CHORIZO and/or
peppers. Eggs may be
added to many vegetable,
pork or game mixtures, or
have additions like prawns
or chopped tomato.
◆◆◆ Huevos a la flamenca
An egg dish of many colours,
hence the name. A tomato
and vegetable sauce goes in
a casserole, then the eggs,
which may be topped with
ham, CHORIZO and prawns,
before baking (see recipe
page 98).
◆ Huevos a la gitanilla
Gypsy eggs, baked in a
purée of bread, almonds
ground with cumin, and
garlic.
Huevos rellenos
Popular stuffed hard-boiled
eggs, often with tuna or
anchovy (*de anchoa*).

decorated with eggs, and
sometimes containing sausage.

Horno
Oven.

Hortelana
The adjective 'vegetable' from
huerta (the 'vegetable plot'). It
often indicates vegetables as
garnish – uncommon in Spain.

Huesos
Bones.

Huesos de santo
'Saint's bones', for All Saints.
Once these were deep-fried
potato pastries, stuffed with
custard, but now they are made
of marzipan.

Huevas
Fish roes. Often *aliñadas*
(marinated) or *fritas*, made into
crisp fritters.

◆◆ Huevas prensadas
Salted pressed tuna roe.

Huevo
Egg. An egg may be *pasado
por agua*, boiled – when it will
be very soft and served in a
wine glass. You peel it, drop it
back in and eat with a spoon.
Huevos estrellados are fried
and sunny side up. *Escalfados*
are poached, and *fritos* fried or
deep-fried; the latter are puffy
and excellent.

I

◆◆ Idiazábal, queso de
Pride of the Basque country, this
hard pressed ewes' milk cheese
is shaped like a small drum.
Smoked ones are stronger, with
toffee-coloured rinds.

◆◆◆ Intxaursalsa
A Basque walnut cream, eaten
chilled on Christmas Eve.

J

◆◆ Jabalí
Boar, found in north and
southern Spain. *Estofado*
(stewed) and *a la montañesa*
both mean with herbs and
onion.

Jamón
For Spain's famous raw ham, see
SERRANO. Cooked ham on the
bone is called *jamón de York*.
Lean slices are often called
MAGRE. Lesser hams are made
with shoulder (*fiambre de
paleta*).

◆◆ Jamón al jerez
Braised ham in sherry.

◆ Jamón con melón o higos
Sliced ham with melon or figs.

Japuta
Pomfret (fish). An excellent fish
– though this nickname means
'son of a bitch'; see PALOMETA.

◆◆ Jarabe
Syrup made from fresh fruit.
Excellent over crushed ice.

Jarrete de ternera
A shin bone of veal made into
some tasty stews.

◆◆ Jibia
Another name for cuttlefish, see
SEPIA. Excellent *en salsa* – in a
sauce with saffron and cumin.

Judías
Dried beans. *Judías pintas*
('painted beans') are the
speckled brown borlotti beans.

◆◆◆ Judías a lo tío Lucas
A popular Madrid dish of mildly
spiced beans. The Uncle Luke
of the title invented it in Cádiz to
feed the half-starved sailors
waiting to be paid off at the end
of voyages.

Judías verdes
Green beans. *Con salsa de*

tomate are with tomato sauce, *con jamón*, with ham. They are cooked with TOCINO and CHORIZO in Madrid.

Julivert
The lovely Catalan word for parsley.

Jurel
Horse mackerel (fish), related to CHICHARRO.

K

◆◆◆ Kokotxas, cocochas
Triangular throat pieces from the hake, and a Basque speciality. Delicious as tiny fritters (*fritas*), they also garnish fish dishes, but are a bit gelatinous cooked with oil and garlic as *pil-pil*.

Koskera
See MERLUZA A LA VASCA.

L

◆◆◆ Lacón con grelos
A hearty Galician soup-stew of cured pork knuckle with the young leaf tops and flower buds of turnips, plus new potatoes.

Lamprea
Lamprey (fish).

◆◆ Langosta
The tiny-clawed rock lobster, called crawfish in Britain and crayfish in the US. Often served cold with mayonnaise; it is served hot in a spicy tomato sauce *al estilo de Bilbao*, or in rice.

◆◆◆ Langosta a la Costa Brava
Crawfish in tomato sauce

flavoured with sweet RANCIO wine and brandy, and thickened with almonds and hazelnuts.

◆◆◆ Langosta con pollo
A Catalan mixture of lobster and chicken, in a SOFRITO-based tomato stew, thickened with a PICADA.

◆◆◆ Langostinos
Big deep-water prawns. Perhaps the best prawn – boiled or cooked simply *a la plancha* (on the hot iron) and served dressed *a la vinagreta* or with pungent ALIOLI. They are also cooked in white wine (*a la marinera*).

Laurel, hojas de
Bay leaves.

◆◆ Lebrada de progonaos
Stewed hare in wine. Like the French *civet*, it includes the animal's blood, but in the Spanish version the sauce is thickened with pine nuts.

◆◆◆ Lechal, lechazo
A milk-fed lamb. A glory when roasted.

◆◆ Leche, arroz con
Cold, milky rice pudding, flavoured with lemon zest. A speciality in the northwest. Sometimes it has a grilled sugar topping (*quemado*).

◆◆ Leche frita
Literally 'fried milk', these hot or cold squares of stiff custard are creamy inside, with a crisp crust from being egg-and-crumbed, then fried. Found in the north.

◆◆ Lechecillas de ternera
Calf's sweetbreads. Popularly made into a stew, which may also include the liver and lights.

◆◆◆ Lechona asada
Roast suckling pig.

Lechuga
Lettuce. Usually a salad, but also

cooked. *Cogolos* (hearts) may be floured and fried, and are sometimes mixed with other hot vegetables.

Legumbres
Pulses, fresh or dried.

Lengua
Tongue in the singular will be an ox tongue, in the plural, lambs' tongues.

◆◆ Lengua estofada
Braised tongue with vegetables, served hot. In Mallorca, pomegranate juice may be included.

◆◆ Lenguado
Sole. It is fried simply, coated with flour or crumbs, for example *a la gaditana*. In Madrid and the Basque country, it is often paired with wine and mushrooms; in Andalucía, where tiny single-person ones are common, with tomatoes and peppers.

Lentejas
Lentils. They are made into soup (*sopa*) or stewed (*cocido*). *A la zamorana*, they are cooked with MORCILLA, garlic and paprika.

Lemons, redolent of the warm south

Levadura
Both baking powder and yeast.

Liadillos
'Tied up', and so stuffed meat or cabbage rolls.

◆◆ Liebre
Hare. Mostly *guisada* or *en su salsa* (stewed with herbs). Red wine is a common addition, with nutmeg, and the sauce is thickened with the liver.

Lima
Lime.

Limanda
Lemon sole.

Limón
Lemon.

◆◆◆ Lisa
The best of the grey mullets. Eat it grilled or baked, for it is fairly oily, but has a good flavour and is easy to bone. It is often cooked like LUBINA and is excellent with saffron sauce (*en amarillo*), on the south coast.

Liscos
A TORTILLA with streaky bacon.

Ll
In Spain this is a separate letter of the alphabet, listed after L.

◆◆◆ Llagosta a la catalana
A Catalan lobster dish with a

sauce of peppers, tomato, wine and brandy. Sometimes it includes chocolate and almonds.

Llampuga
Catalan for DORADA.

Llauna, a la
Catalan for 'in a metal oven dish', ie baked.

◆◆◆ Llegumet
A thick dish with beans, rice *and* potatoes, in Alicante, including snails.

Locha
Small cod or loach.

Locro
Stew with maize.

◆ Lombardo
Red cabbage. Cooked *a San Isidro* is with bacon and potatoes, or with apples and wine.

Lomo
Loin. Notably pork loin, much eaten in Spain. It may be pot roast with sherry or sweet Málaga wine, or stuffed (*relleno*) with nuts, ham or SOBRASADA sausage.

Lomo bajo
Sirloin or loin of beef.

◆ Lomo de cerdo a la zaragozano
Pork loin cooked with ham, onions, wine and tomatoes, and the local chopped black olives.

◆◆ Lomo de cerdo con leche
Pork loin pot-roast in milk.

◆◆◆ Lomo embuchado
Smoked, pink pork loin cured whole in a sausage casing. It tastes like good ham. A *caña de lomo* is also a cured loin.

◆ Longaniza
A sausage, remarkable for its length, and sometimes fresh. Also a rather bland, hard, thin salami sausage, which hangs in a hank, wrapped around a wooden rod.

Lonja
Thick slice.

◆◆◆ Lubina
Sea bass. One of the finest fish, best when line-caught. Baked *Costa Brava* style with red wine and onions, poached or grilled, it is exceptional. *A la asturiana* it is cooked in cider (or white wine) with clams or mussels and possibly potatoes.

◆◆◆ Lubina Albufera
From the great Valencian freshwater lake, this sea bass is served with ground almond and paprika sauce.

Lucio
Pike.

M

Maccarones
Macaroni. Served with cheese sauce, and also chicken giblet dressing.

Macedonia de frutas
Fruit salad.

◆◆ Machacón
Boiled potatoes dressed with chopped tomato and pepper, plus oil and often cumin.

Macis
Mace (part of nutmeg).

Maduro
Ripe.

Magdalenas
Sponge cup cakes, from the French *madeleines*.

◆◆ Magro
'Lean', usually pork. *Magras con tomate* is fried ham in tomato sauce. It is also served in sweet sauces of Málaga wine, or with cherries.

◆◆ Mahón, queso de
A well-regarded, flattish square cheese, semi-hard with a tangy

taste. It is made from cows' milk in Menorca.

Mahonesa, mayonesa
Two words for mayonnaise, the first reflecting the belief it was invented at Mahón (Maó) on Menorca.

Maiz
Maize or sweetcorn.

◆ Málaga, queso de
A goats' milk cheese, matured for just five days.

Mamia
Basque junket; see CUAJADA.

◆◆◆ Manchego, queso de
Spain's Cheddar cheese. Made from ewes' milk, it is sold at various stages from semi-hard, when it is mild, to *añejo* (aged) which is sharp, hard and reminiscent of Parmesan. The waxed rind bears the mark of the rope mould, and the black drum form is best known, though some rinds are yellowish; colour does not indicate age.

Mandarina
Tangerine.

◆ Manos de cerdo, manitas
Trotters. They are cooked until the fat jellies, with beans or chick-peas (*con judías o garbanzos*) to absorb the fat. For *manitas rehogadas*, they are boned out and stuffed, then egged, crumbed and fried.

◆◆ Manteca colora
Paprika-flavoured pork fat. A bread-spread that may also include shreds of meat, like French *rillettes;* a good starter.

◆◆ Mantecados
Rich, crumbly little 'lardy cakes' that often include ground almonds. The ones from Astorga in León are famous.

Mantequilla
Butter.

Preparing for the next catch

◆ Manzanas asadas
Baked apples or *rellenas* (stuffed), good if the stuffing is chestnut.

Manzanillas
Common small green olives.

◆◆◆ Mar i terra or mar i muntanya
Dishes that combine 'seafood' with chicken 'from the mountain'. Most glamorous is chicken with lobster in a saffron, hazelnut and chocolate sauce.

Maragota
Wrasse (fish). With coarse and somewhat insipid flesh, it mainly goes in soups. It can be stuffed and baked (*al horno*).

Mariscos
Shellfish.
◆◆◆ **Marmitako**
A Basque shipboard stew,
which takes its name from the
cooking pot (the French
marmite). It is made from BONITO
(white tuna) and whole new
potatoes in a piquant, puréed
red pepper sauce.
Marrajo
Porbeagle shark. Good grilled;
see CAILÓN.
◆◆ **Marrons glacés**
Much more sugary than the
crystallised French chestnuts.
Maruca
Spanish ling and the largest

Seafood in its infinite variety

member of the cod family. It
cooks more like whiting, so
needs pepping up.
Masa
Bread dough or pastry.
Mat mulo
Very fresh. Literally 'the mule
killer', it refers to the speed with
which fish is rushed inland.
◆ **Mataero, ajo de**
A very similar dish to
MORTERUELO, with pork, bacon,
liver and pine kernels.
Matalahuva, (matalahuga)
Aniseed (aniseed plant).
◆◆◆ **Matanza**
A big event in the peasant
food year, when the pig is
killed by a *matador*, some
time in November after All
Saints. The sequence of
dishes starts with liver and
brains on the first day, and a
splendid meal! Many sausages
are made with the offal and
blood.
Mató
Fresh goats' milk cheese.
◆ **Mazapán**
Marzipan. It is made into
figuritas, little animals, shapes
and Christmas figures.
◆◆◆ **Mejillones**
Mussels. They are often
included in fish sauces, soups
and PAELLA. They are served
cold on the shell (*a la vinagreta*)
or baked (*al horno*), they are
also good fried in breadcrumbs
(*empanados*).
◆◆ **Mejillones a la marinera**
Mussels opened in white wine
with onion, garlic and oil.
Mejorana
Marjoram. Sweeter than
oregano.
◆◆ **Mel i mató**
Fresh cream cheese served
with honey (MIEL).

Melaza
Molasses.
Melindres
'Lady-finger' biscuits, sometimes marzipan.
Melocotón
Peach.
◆◆ Melocotón en almíbar
Peaches in syrup, from Arab times.
◆◆◆ Melocotónes asados en vino tinto
Peaches baked in red wine.
Melón
Melon. Honeydews and Piel de Sapo are celebrated.
◆◆◆ Melón con jamón
Melon with raw SERRANO ham.
◆◆◆ Membrillo
Quince. Popular as a stewed fruit, but most of all as a stiff, sweet, pink paste, sold as *dulce, flan* or even *carne de membrillo;* good with hard cheese.
◆◆◆ Menestra de Tudela
Asparagus stewed with other vegetables.
◆ Menestra de verduras
A vegetable stew. At its most attractive when it is a mixture of boiled with fried vegetables. Chopped hard-boiled eggs are added, and many versions include ham. *Menestra a la asturiana* includes fried potatoes and ham, while *extremeña* is based on potatoes and greens. *Menestra de pollo* includes chicken.
◆◆ Menjar blanco
Means 'white eat' and is a creamy ground almond dessert with lemon juice. It once included pounded chicken breasts.
Menta
Mint.
Menudillos
Chicken giblets. Common in

rice dishes, baked with eggs and in tomato sauce.
Menudos
Offal.
◆ Menudos gitanos
Gypsy tripe, cooked with ham, chick-peas, garlic, saffron and cumin, also called *callos a la andaluza*.
Merengues
Meringues.
Merlano
Whiting. It has light white flesh, but is a rather tasteless fish.
Merlo
Wrasse (fish). Used in soup.
◆◆ Merluza
Hake. Spain's most popular and plentiful fish: fine-flavoured and flaky. It is cooked in cider (*a la sidra*), with capers (*alcaparras*), with potatoes (*gallega*) and is good cold (*con mayonesa*).
◆◆ Merluza a la vasca
Hake with white wine sauce, clams and prawns and sometimes asparagus tips or eggs (see recipe page 105).
◆◆◆ Merluza en salsa verde
Hake in a sauce made green with parsley. It has an onion base and contains clams, prawns and even KOKOTXAS. Its other names include *merluza bibaina* and *cazuela Santander*.
Mermelada
A thick, compote-like jam of any flavour. Try peach or plum jam; berries are less good.
Marmalade is *mermelada de naranja*.
◆◆◆ Mero
Grouper (fish). One of Spain's most delicious fish, it is lean and flaky. A versatile fish, it is good *al horno*, baked with white wine and potatoes, grilled, or served hot in orange sauce, and cold, *en vinagreta*.

◆◆ Michirones
Broad beans stewed with
CHORIZO and chilli.

Miel
Honey. Best from one flower,
like orange flower (*miel de
azahar*).

Mielga
Spur dog shark. One of the best
edible sharks; see CAILÓN.

◆◆ Miera cielo
This 'heavenly dish' is a roast
red pepper salad, with slivers of
dry roast salted cod in olive oil.

◆◆◆ Migas
Fried breadcrumbs or small
croûtons. They give texture to
many egg, bacon and vegetable
dishes and make a dessert with
chocolate sauce or grapes.

Migas canas
A savoury bread pudding of
MIGAS with milk, and often
bacon.

Mijo
Millet.

Modroñes
Arbutus. The fruit of the
strawberry tree, pretty but not
particularly good to eat.

Traditional cork oak beehives

◆ Moixernon
The earliest wild mushroom –
'St George's'.

◆◆ Mojama
The dark, salted back of the
blue fin tuna. It is a luxury.

Mojarra
The two-banded bream.
Excellent grilled or baked; see
DENTÓN.

◆◆ Mojete
A simple salad of strips of cold
roasted onions and peppers,
dressed with lemon juice, garlic
and oil, and sometimes cumin.
Salted cod or sardines may also
be included. It is eaten with
bread, not forks.

◆◆◆ Mojo colorado
A cold emulsion of paprika and
cumin with chilli, oil and
vinegar. Served with hot fish in
the Canary Isles. The green
mojo verde uses fresh coriander
leaves – rare in Spain.

◆◆ Mollejas
Sweetbreads. Often stewed in
wine with onion and ham.

Mongetes, monjetes
Dried white beans served with
BUTIFARRA.

Montañesa, a la
From Santander, where the
surrounding green region is
known as 'the Mountain'.

Mora
Mulberry.

◆◆ Moraga de sardinas
A 'bundle' of fresh sardines
casseroled with olive oil, wine,
garlic, lemon and parsley.

◆◆◆ Morcilla
A black sausage including rice
or onions, pigs' blood and often
oregano. The best come from
Asturias and are smoked. There
is also a sweet *morcilla dulce*,
sliced and eaten for *tapas*.

◆ Morcón
Ham made from the shoulder or
other pork offcuts, well spiced.

Morena
The pleasant white flesh of the
Moray eel. It is often found in
fish stews; see CALDERETA.

◆ Moreno
A small shaped almond
meringue, which is twice
baked.

Moros y cristianos
A dish of black beans and white
rice, commemorating an old
conflict between Moors and
Christians.

Morro
Cheek. Usually pork. Often
stewed with beans. Calf's cheek
is a rarity, usually braised.

◆◆ Morteruelo
A hot hash of mixed meats
including game and pounded
liver, or a cold terrine, spiced
with cumin.

◆ Mostachones
S-shaped biscuits, often with
nuts, which combine in pairs to
make a 'moustache'.

Mostaza
Mustard.

Mujol, múgil
The lesser grey mullet. It is
cooked like LISA, but is famous
for its cured roe.

Musclos
Usually chicken legs. Also
Catalan for mussel.

Musola
The smooth-hound, a
good-to-eat shark; see CAZÓN.

N

Nabo
Turnip, *naps* in Catalan.

◆ Naranja
Orange. Excellent with raw
onions as a starter (*ensalada de
naranja*). *Naranjas
acarame[izadas* is a salad, in
caramel syrup. Oranges make a
delicious sorbet (*sorbete*).

Nata
Cream. Uncommon in the south,
and kept for desserts, like
whipped cows' cream flavoured
with cinnamon, sugar and
lemon, or with nuts or fruit.

◆◆ Natillas
Rich custards made with many
egg yolks, cinnamon and lemon
zest. Excellent when served
very cold. Sometimes the whites
are served as accompanying
meringues.

◆ Navajas
Long, brown razorshell clams,
Eaten raw or steamed.

◆ Nécoras
Small shore crabs. Served
boiled or in soups.

◆ Niscalo
The 'bleeding' or saffron milk
cap. Spain's most picked wild
mushroom; see ROVELLON.

◆ **Nispero**
Loquat. A plum-sized Easter fruit with a double seed, deep-yellow, grainy, sweet flesh and toughish skin.

Ñora
A sweet mild chilli; see ROMESCO.

Nuez
Nut. Commonly means walnut, as in *sopa de nueces* (walnut cream soup) from the walnut tree (*nogal*). *Nueces variados* are mixed unshelled nuts.

Nuez de moscada
Nutmeg.

◆ **Oropesa**
A hard, ewes' milk, Castilian cheese, stored in olive oil.

Ortiga
Stinging nettle.

◆◆◆ **Ostra**
The true oyster. *Ostión* is the cheaper, cultivated so-called Portuguese oyster, a speciality round Cádiz. It is excellent coated and fried (*fritas*) in a *tartera*, with garlic and breadcrumbs, or in SOPA DEL CUARTO DE HORA.

Ous
Catalan for egg.

O

Oca
Young goose.

◆◆ **Oca con peras**
A gosling cooked with pears.

Olla
The cooking pot; see PUCHERO. *Olla gitana*, a 'gypsy pot', includes any vegetable, with fruit, such as pears. *Olleta* is another vegetable pot; in Valencia it may include game.

◆◆ **Olla podrida**
Literally means 'rotten pot', because the meat is simmered so long it has the softness of overripe fruit.

Orégano
Oregano.

Orejas
Pigs' ears. Often salted and popular eaten with beans.

Orejones
Dried apricots. Strung up in a ring, hence the name 'ears'.

◆ **Orelletes**
'Little ears' of twisted *anís*-flavoured pastry, deep-fried, served with sugar or honey.

P

◆◆◆ **Pa amb tomàquet**
A do-it-yourself snack, served at most Catalan meals, this is toast with tomato juice squeezed over. Olive oil finishes it off and sometimes SERRANO and cheese are put on top.

Pa d'ous
Catalan for FLAN (custard dessert).

◆◆◆ **Paella a la valenciana**
The original *paella*, of saffron rice, with a mixture of chicken or rabbit, fish, prawns and shellfish, with peppers. There are many versions and the shellfish *paella de mariscos* is also popular in Valencia. *A la catalana* includes sausage, pork and peppers.

◆◆ **Paella al estilo de Parellada**
Named after Juli Parellada, a 19th-century dandy, who asked for his *paella* 'without bones or shells' in.

Pagès
'From the countryside'. *Pan de pagès* is very solid bread.

Paire
Long thin scabbard fish. Cut diagonally and grilled.

Pajaritos
Small birds. Eaten less now people are better off.

Paletillo
Shoulder. Used for old-fashioned dishes, like stewed mutton (*de carnero*).

Palitos
A skewer and anything on it, usually a *tapa*.

◆ **Palmeras de hojaldre**
A delicious biscuit consisting of two whirls of puff pastry cut side up – the French *palmiers*.

◆ **Palmito, ensalada de**
Palm heart salad. Usually with pink mayonnaise and lettuce. Fresh *palmetto* is an Easter dish.

Paloma
Dove or pigeon, *torcaz* if wild; see PICHON.

◆◆ **Palometa**
A deep-water fish, *palometa negra* is pomfret (Ray's bream), excellent to eat. The flesh is faintly pink and flakes in long strands like skate. It is good fried and worthy of rich sauces. *Palometa blanco* is pompano.

Palomitas
Popcorn.

Pan
White bread, excellent quality in Spain. Catalunya has a three-cornered loaf – which the Surrealist artist Salvador Dali stuck all over the outside of his house! Wholemeal bread is *pan integral*. *Pan rallado* is breadcrumbs.

Pan de centeno
Rye bread, made in Galicia.

◆◆ **Pan de higos**
Sweetmeat of dried figs, in a flat cake like the Italian *panforte*. It

In a Marbella restaurant

is coated underneath with chocolate.

Pan de pernil
Jellied ham.

◆◆ **Panades**
Lamb pies in Mallorca, made at Easter.

Panadons
Catalan word for pasties. They may have spinach or fish like tuna in them.

Panceta
Pork belly with some lean – unlike TOCINO.

Panecicos
Sweet puff made of breadcrumbs with egg white, fried then soaked in syrup.

Panecillos
Bread rolls.

◆◆ **Panellets**
Small sweet cakes, of almond paste, sometimes sweet potato, and topped with pine nuts or

almonds. They are made for All Saints' Day in many flavours.

◆ **Panquemado**
'Burnt bread', a sugar-glazed breakfast bread.

◆◆ **Papas arrugadas**
'Wrinkled potatoes' are new potatoes boiled in seawater until salt-crusted, then baked and served with spicy MOJO sauce. *Papas* is 'potato' in the Canary Isles.

◆ **Pargo**
Sea bream with rosy tints to its side and tail. Excellent as steaks, or stuffed or baked.

Parrilla, a la
From the grill.

◆◆◆ **Parrillada de pescado**
A mixed grill of fish. In Catalunya this may include shellfish too. (*Parrillada* following a noun is a *gratin*.)

Pasas
Dried fruit, usually raisins; famous when from Málaga. *Pasas de corinto* are currants, while CIRUELAS PASAS are prunes.

◆ **Pasiego, queso de**
A fresh soft cheese, made into a cheesecake in Santander; used to make QUESADA.

Pasta quebrada
Flaky pastry.

Pastel
Embraces even more food than the American term 'pie'. In most of Spain, it is the word for a pastry-topped pie. *Pastel de conejo* is rabbit pie and *pastel de pescado* fish pie. Also the common word for cake, and any solid, cooked pudding.

Pastel de berenjenas
An aubergine terrine or timbale.

Pastel de higado
Liver pâté.

Pastel de pasas
A rather soggy breadcrumb and raisin pudding. The similar *pastel de Pascua* (Easter pudding) in Mallorca is made with eggs and biscuit crumbs.

◆ **Pasteles de carne**
Pasties enclosing savoury meat, perhaps with chopped egg (to absorb juice) and vegetables. *Pastel murciano* is a spicy version. There are also potato cakes including chopped sausage.

Pastelvasco
See GATAVASK.

Pastillas
Pastilles (sweets). The milk-and-coffee caramels of Logroño are well known.

Pata
Foot. *Patas de cerdo a la parrilla* are grilled trotters.

◆ **Patacó, patacu**
A casserole of tuna with potato, sometimes containing snails. It can be adapted to pork.

Patatas
Potato. Diced potatoes are 'hazelnutted' (*avellanada*).

◆ **Patatas a la riojana**
Potatoes flavoured (and coloured) with CHORIZO.

◆◆ **Patatas bravas**
A popular *tapa* of potatoes in a spicy tomato sauce – very spicy in Barcelona.

◆ **Patatas castellanas**
Potatoes fried with plenty of paprika.

Patatas pobres
'Poor man's potatoes', with garlic and parsley.

Patatas viudas
'Widow's potatoes' with only fried onion.

Pato
Duck. Commonly roast, it is served in the north with turnips (*con nabos*) and in Catalunya with figs, *pato con higos*.

◆◆ Pato a la sevillana
The original 'duck with orange'
from Seville, it does not taste of
orange. The acidity of the bitter
fruit, plus olives, cuts the fat of
the pot-roast bird. *Pato con
aceitunas* (duck with olives) is
very similar.
Pavías de pescado
Fish fingers; see SOLDADITOS DE
PAVÍA.
Pavo
Turkey. They are smaller in
Spain and you may find breasts
or roast birds stuffed with
apples or chestnuts.
◆◆ Pebre, en, all-i-pebre
In 'pepper', ie paprika. This 'oil
and pepper' sauce is very
simple but good for eels
(ANGUILAS), fish and chicken.
Pecho de cerdo
Belly of pork.
◆ Pechuga de pollo
Chicken breast. These may be
stuffed (*rellena*), crumbed
(*empanada*) and are excellent
with orange sauce (*en salsa de
naranja*).
◆ Pelotas, pilotas
Small meatballs, poached in
broth like dumplings.
Pencas
Usually the stalks of ACELGA
(Swiss chard), without the leaf.
Pepino
Cucumber. Mainly used as a
plain salad. *Pepinillos* are
pickled gherkins.
Pepitas
Seeds for snacks: sunflower or
melon seeds.
**◆ Pepitoria de gallina (or de
pollo)**
A fricassee of hen or chicken
with a distinctive Arab ground
almond and garlic sauce.
Peras
Pears.

**◆ Peras al horno or al vino
tinto**
Pears baked with red wine and
cinnamon.
Perca
Perch.
◆◆ Percebes
A very expensive shellfish, a
speciality of Galicia, usually
translated as a 'goose-neck
barnacle'. It looks like a
miniature bear's claw with
white fingernails, and tastes
of the sea.
Perdices a la capellán
The 'chaplain's partridges' are
not birds, but beef rolls with
ham and SOBRASADO inside.
**Perdiz, perdices, perdigones,
perdiú**
Partridge(s).

Apples and pears come from Asturias

Partridge – A Popular Country Dish
This is a familiar dish for country folk all over Spain. Usually pot-roast with a little wine, it is also good *amb rovellon* (with wild mushrooms); see also ESCABECHE.

◆◆◆ Perdices a la torero
Bull-fighters are well fed and these partridges are braised with ham, tomatoes, wine and anchovies.

◆◆◆ Perdices al chocolate
Partridges with chocolate. Found all over Spain; not sweet at all, but a rich, dark gravy.

◆◆ Perdices con coles
Partridges rolled in cabbage leaves.

Perejil
Parsley. In Spain it is flat-leaved and mild. It garnishes salads and goes into a PICADA and an ALIÑO.

◆◆ Pericana
A salted cod salad which includes crumbled pieces of fried, dried red chilli, in Valencia. It is served with COCA.

Pernil
The Catalan word for SERRANO.

Perol
A deep frying pan, used for soupy rice dishes.

Perros y gatos
'Dogs and cats' – ugly fish sold under a pet name.

◆ Perruñillas, perruñas
Sweet, cinnamon 'dog biscuits'. They bake with deep cracks. *Perruñas* are richer, flavoured with lemon zest and are coated with egg white and sugar.

◆◆ Pescadillo
The small silver hake (sometimes called whiting). This fish is less flat than many others, with fillets on top of the backbone, so it is served belly down. Larger ones are deep fried in a ring, with the tail in the mouth (*se come su cola*). Smaller ones make soup; see CALDILLO.

Pescado
Fish.

◆◆◆ Pescaíto frito.
Fried fish, a star *tapa* in Cádiz.

◆◆ Pestiños, pistiñes
A sweet fritter of *anís* or wine pastry, made by overlapping the opposite corners of a square. Deep-fried until they puff, they are soaked in syrup and served with sugar or honey.

Pez angel
Angelfish shark; see ANGELOTE.

◆◆◆ Pez espada
Swordfish. The flesh is firm, almost meaty and consequently expensive; steaks are grilled, though they can be a little dry. It may be cooked like ATÚN and is good *en* AMARILLO (in a yellow sauce).

◆ Pez limón
Amberjack, the fish with a long yellow streak. It is good grilled, baked, or as fried fillets served in sauce.

Pez martillo
Hammerhead shark. Small ones make good eating.

Picada
The final addition to a sauce that thickens it. In Catalunya it is made of garlic, bread and toasted nuts.

Picadillo
'Chopped small', so usually means minced meat. *Picadillos* is a hash, and includes sausage when used for stuffing.

Pescaíto frito – *mixed fried fish*

Picante
Spicy hot. GUINDILLA is the only
Spanish chilli to fear.
◆ Picatostes
Fried bread fingers or buttered
toast, often sugared.
Pichón
Pigeon or squab. Probably
pot-roast with a little wine.
**◆◆◆ Pichón con pasas y
piñones**
Pigeon with raisins and pine
nuts in a sherry or sweet wine
sauce.
◆◆◆ Picón, queso de
A creamy blue cheese, named
for its home in the Picos de
Europa; see CABRALES.
◆◆◆ Pierna
Leg, often roast. Lamb is *de
cordera; a la oransana* it is
cooked on top of haricot beans,
like the French *boulangère*.
Roast kid (*pierna de cabrito*) is
also delicious.
Pies
Feet; see PATA.
Pijama
The best dessert in the house: a
FLAN and an ice, or two sorts of

ice-cream, with three types of
canned fruit is typical. It used to
mean 'covered in whipped
cream', and this is where the
'pyjamas' (formerly nightshirts)
came in.
Pijotas
Baby hake. They are crisp-fried
on the south coast.
Pilongas
Dried chestnuts. Made into a
puréed soup or stewed with
beans and pork.
◆◆◆ Pil-pilando
A sizzling dish; see GAMBAS
PIL-PIL. One of the rare dishes
served extremely hot, for
Spanish food is often just warm.
It has no connection with the
white Basque sauce called
pil-pil.
Pimentón
Paprika, a basic pepper in
Spain.
Pimienta
Black pepper.
Pimientos
Peppers.

A–Z FOOD GUIDE

A mainstay of Spanish cooking

Peppers: Popular Sweet or Spicy Vegetables

◆◆◆ **Pimientos de piquillo rellenos de bacalao**
A Basque speciality of spicy, long red peppers, stuffed with salted cod, then fried and served in a sauce.

◆◆ **Pimientos fritos**
Small deep-fried green peppers. Popular all over Spain, the best are from Padrón.

◆◆ **Pimientos rellenos**
Stuffed peppers. Usually the familiar fat ones, with ham or pork.

◆◆◆ **Pimientos rojos asados**
Roast, skinned red peppers, served as a salad with oil; very Spanish!

◆◆ **Pinchitos morunos**
Small pork kebabs, flavoured with cumin and coriander.

Pinchos
Any food that can be skewered on a cocktail stick, almost synonymous with *tapas*.

◆◆ **Piñonatas**
Expensive, rich-tasting little pine nut cakes.

Piñones
Pine nuts. Tiny and cream-coloured, they are extracted from the cones of stone pines, and are consequently expensive. The flavour is astringent, yet rich, much liked for sauces, vegetable dishes and cakes.

Pintada
Guinea fowl. Mainly roast in smart restaurants.

Pintarroja
A dogfish or small shark. Good to eat; see CAZÓN.

Pipas
Seeds. White sunflower seeds (*de girasol*) are a common snack, but pumpkin (*pipas calabazo*) and melon seeds are also sold, often in mixed packets with salted peanuts and sweetcorn.

Piperita
Peppermint.

◆◆◆ **Piperrada**
A soft, creamy omelette in the French style, flavoured with puréed roast red pepper, onions and tomatoes. *Piperra* is the Basque word for 'pepper', and dishes containing them.

◆◆ **Pipirrana**
A salad of chopped peppers, tomato, cucumber and onion. Served very cold, this is close to GAZPACHO. It may contain BACALAO or tuna, with a dressing based on hard egg yolks; in Jaén it is served with SERRANO.

◆◆ Piriñaca
A salad of mixed chopped vegetables without cucumber. The same mixture accompanies baked fish, such as *besugo asado con piriñaca*.

◆◆◆ Pisto
A tomato, aubergine and mixed vegetable sauce, meaning a 'hotchpotch'. *Pisto manchego* includes scrambled egg. Good with fish too (*pisto de peces*).

Pixin
Monkfish; see RAPE.

Plancha, a la
On the hot iron (griddle): a way of grilling with very little oil.

Plátanos
Bananas.

◆◆◆ Plátanos fritos
Fried bananas. Popular in the Canary Islands.

Platija
Flounder (fish); the name means 'flat'. Good to eat.

Pochas
Haricot beans. Eaten fresh.

◆◆◆ Pochas con codornices
Fresh haricots cooked with quail. The dish opens the hunting season.

◆◆ Pochas riojanas
Fresh haricots cooked with CHORIZO, which reddens the podded beans.

Poleo
Type of mint.

◆◆◆ Pollastre amb gambes
Catalan chicken with prawns, in a red wine and pine nut sauce.

Pollo
Chicken. *Rebozado* it is coated with breadcrumbs and fried. *Al jerez*, it is finished with sherry and *a la granadina*, it includes raw ham too. *Pollo con aceitunas* is stewed gently with green olives. *Pollo en arroz* (chicken in rice) is common on the north coast; see CAMPURRIANO.

◆◆ Pollo al chilindrón
Chicken cooked with peppers, tomatoes and onions. *Pollo en chanfaina* is similar; see SAMFAINA.

◆◆ Pollo asado
Spanish chickens are often roast with pork fat, salt and paprika, which makes their skin wonderfully tasty. Also good roast *con salsa de naranja* (basted with orange juice).

◆◆◆ Polvorones
'Crumble cakes'. As this is what these little cakes do very easily, they are paper-wrapped. The best ones include ground almonds as well as flour and sugar, flavoured with *anís* and cinnamon. They are made all over Spain, but those from Antequera are outstanding. Accompany them with a glass of *anís* or OLOROSO sherry.

Pomelo
Grapefruit.

◆◆◆ Porchella asado
Roast suckling pig in Mallorca.

◆◆ Porra antequerana
A very thick type of GAZPACHO with raw ham.

Postre
Like the English 'afters', it means dessert.

Postre de músico
A Christmas dish of nuts and dried fruits.

◆ Potaje
A thick vegetable soup – pottage. *Potaje de valenciana* has chick-peas and spinach, *potaje murciana* has rice, green beans and FRIJOLES (dried beans).

◆◆ Pote asturiana
A thick soup of beans and sausage. *Pote primavera* is a

mix of spring vegetables. *Pote granadina* contains tomato, peppers and onions, probably with saffron.

◆ Poti poti
Salted cod salad, with potatoes and peppers.

Pringadas
Fried bread, often with bacon or sausage. The name comes from a verb that means 'to fry in bacon fat'.

Puchero
An earthenware cooking pot, and so a stew. The Andalucían *puchero* usually contains a wide range of vegetables and even tomato sauce, while in the Canary Isles, *puchero canario* has pumpkin, sweetcorn, sweet potato, even pears.

Pudín
Like English pudding, it can take lots of forms, including anything moulded. It can mean a cold meat or fish mould, even a hot meat loaf! In Mallorca, it is a cold egg and bread pudding.

Puerro
Leek.

Pulpeta
A slice of meat; it may be rolled with a filling.

Pulpo
Octopus. *Pulpitas* are baby ones and likely to be more tender.

◆◆◆ Pulpo al feria
A famous Galician dish of boiled octopus served in a paprika-oil dressing. This is usually a salad, but might come hot from the pot.

Puntillitas
Small squid. Fried in batter as a *tapa*.

◆◆ Purrusalda, porrosaldo
A Basque leek and potato soup. This usually includes cooked BACALAO.

◆ Puzol, queso de
A fresh cows' milk cheese in Valencia, moulded with a conical indent.

Q

Quemada
'Burnt', that is topped with caramelised sugar. Sweet bread and ice-cream prepared this way are both good.

Quesada, quesadilla
Cheesecake.

Queso
Cheese.

◆◆ Queso frito
Fried cheese. Slices are egged and breadcrumbed then fried.

Quisquilla
The common prawn.

R

◆◆ Raba
A north coast squid dish, bread-coated, then fried.

Rábano
Red radish. *Rábano picante* is the stronger horseradish.

◆◆◆ Rabo de toro estofado
Bull's tail, slow-stewed with onions and tomatoes, or with sherry (*al jerezana*).

Rana, ancas de
Frogs' legs. Fried with garlic and parsley.

◆ Rancho canario
A stew in the Canary Isles with dried beans, potatoes and pasta, plus a little CHORIZO and bacon.

◆ Rape
Monkfish. Hugely popular in Spain. It is fried with paprika

Spanish Cheese

Basically Spanish cheese is either hard or very fresh. Compared with France, Spain lacks the whole middle range of matured creamy cheeses.

However, mountains (of which Spain has plenty) and cheese go together, because they support cows and sheep. From their milk come a range of unusual hand-made cheeses, mainly using unpasteurised milk. There are a few semi-hard cheeses, like CANTABRIA and MAHÓN, but it is the hard cheeses that mature to distinction. Most famous of them all is MANCHEGO. Like most Spanish hard cheeses, it passes from mild when semi-hard, to strong and sharp when hard. RONCAL is another that matures. Some hard cheese is stored in olive oil, which allows it to mature without drying out: attractive examples are from Oropesa and those exported from Burgos by Gúzman. Two well known smoked cheeses are IDIAZÁBAL and SAN SIMÓN. Creamy blue cheeses are made, much in the same style as Roquefort, like *cabarales* and the similar PICÓN.

Hard and soft cheese bear

Spain's best known cheese

the marks of rope moulds. The wrapping (like a Dick Whittington bundle) shows up on the Levantine *servilleta*, while PUZOL has a conical depression in the middle.

Soft cottage cheeses (REQUESÓNES) are made all over the country, and soft fresh cheeses, like the ewes' milk BURGOS, which is widely available, or the similar CERVERA. Other local cheeses are VILLALÓN and MÁLAGA. Spain has no long tradition of cooking with cheese – it is mostly eaten with bread before or after a meal. However, the hard cheeses grate well.

(*en pimentón*) in the south. *Al estilo de Costa Brava*, it is stewed with tomatoes, red peppers, white wine and fresh peas. Cold, it makes an excellent salad (*ensalada*).

Rascacio

Rascasse (fish). It is a favourite for fish soups and stocks, but can be cooked like DENTÓN.

◆◆ Raspas de anchoas

Anchovy backbones, deep-fried

for a *tapa*. It sounds terrible, but is actually crunchy and tasty.

Raya
The wingflaps of skates (the ray shark). Good to eat, for the flesh falls from the bones in attractive strips: especially good with something acid like capers or lemon juice. Skate is marinated then served *en adobo* in the south.

◆ **Raya en pimentón**
Skate wings cooked with paprika.

Rebanada
Slice, eg of bread. *Rebañar* means 'to wipe round the plate' – it is good manners here not to leave food on the plate.

Rebeco
Chamoix.

Rebozado
Battered – 'hidden in a shawl' – and deep fried.

◆ **Recuit**
A soft fresh cheese, eaten with honey or sugar.

Redondo
Part of the beef rump, tied and roasted in a joint.

Rellena
'Stuffed'. From peppers (usually the slim, hot ones) to red cabbage to pig's trotters; fillings are often meat and sausage.

◆◆ **Remojón**
A BACALAO salad, the name means 'soaked', for this is how the fish is prepared. There are several versions: one with oranges, another with peppers, potatoes, olives and hard-boiled eggs.

Rémol
Brill (fish). It is cooked like RODABALLO.

Remolacha
Beetroot.

Reo
Sea trout, formerly called salmon trout because of its pink flesh. Cooked like SALMÓN.

Repápalos
A version of bread and milk, little balls of egg and crumbs are fried, then served in milk and cinnamon.

Repollo
Drumhead cabbage.

◆ **Requesón**
Smooth cottage cheese, often bearing pretty mould marks. In Madrid, cheeses from Miraflores and El Paular are traditional.

◆◆◆ **Revuelto con ajetes**
Scrambled eggs with green garlic shoots.

◆◆◆ **Revuelto con espárragos trigueros**
Scrambled eggs with wild asparagus: a springtime speciality.

◆◆◆ **Revuelto de setas**
Scrambled eggs with wild mushrooms.

Revueltos
Stirred (ie scrambled) eggs. Unlike TORTILLA, which is a dense egg cake.

Riñonada
Kidneys in their fat, so roasted, or a kidney and other offal mix.

◆◆◆ **Riñones al jerez**
Kidneys in sherry sauce. In poorer areas, this is made with pigs' kidneys and ham in tomato sauce. An excellent dish with veal or lambs' kidneys, and a universal *tapa*.

Rioja, a la
Rioja style. Good red peppers grow in Rioja and paprika is also made. It is odds-on a dish *a la Rioja* will contain them, or red CHORIZO sausage, which include the paprika.

A corner of rural Mallorca

◆ **Robioles**
A small fried Easter pastry that contains custard or CABELLO DE ANGÉL jam.

Rodaballo
Turbot. An expensive fish.

◆◆◆ **Rodaballo al alberiño**
Turbot fillets poached in white wine sauce.

Rollitos
Little rolls, containing cheese, ham, meat or fish. Or sweet ones, like *rollitos de aquardiente* and *rollets*.

Rollo de carne
Meat loaf.

◆◆ **Romana, a la**
Any fish or shellfish battered then deep-fried. Generously, Italy is credited for something done superlatively well in Spain.

Romero
Rosemary.

◆◆◆ **Romesco de pescado**
A fish or shellfish dish on the east coast, sometimes containing dried beans, to which ROMESCO sauce is added before serving.

◆◆◆ **Romesco, salsa**
An exceptional sauce, made of ground toasted almonds and hazelnuts, with the special sweet, mild chilli called *romesco* in the Catalan country. It is excellent with fried fish or roast chicken.

◆ **Roncal, queso de**
A mild, medium-hard ewes' milk cheese, shaped like a small drum. It develops holes the size of rice. Factory made in Navarra, it is well regarded, most of it going to France.

◆◆ **Ropa vieja**
A famous old-fashioned dish – the name means 'old clothes'. When boiled COCIDO was made regularly, next day the left-over meat was served hot in a new sauce, made with peppers, aubergine and tomatoes.

Rosada
The Spanish equivalent of 'rockfish', a name for anonymous

varieties of dogfish (sharks) and a saltwater catfish. Always sold skinned, they are very pink-fleshed. Many are good to eat, but need an acid marinade.

◆◆ Roscon de Reyes
A big Twelfth-Night ring yeast cake, scented with orange-flower water. The flavour and coarse texture are much like the Italian *panettone*. The crust is sprinkled with chopped nuts and fruit, and traditionally it has a single charm hidden in it.

◆ Roscos
Doughnuts. Frequently flavoured with aniseed, they are made in rings and deep-fried. Good ones are made in Burgos. *Rosquillas* are ring-shaped doughnuts or buns, made of batter, rich scone dough or even puff pastry, and usually a generous amount of egg. They are fried or baked, then glazed.

◆ Rosquillas de Alcalá
Pastry rings, frosted twice, first with egg then sugar syrup.

◆ Rosquillas de Santa Clara
Rings dipped in a meringue made with syrup and rebaked.

◆ Rosquillas tontas y listas
'Rich or poor' buns, some iced with sugar, others plain.

Rossejat
An oven rice dish, which often uses leftovers from COCIDO. It is 'browned' by brushing the top with egg.

◆◆ Rovellon
Spain's favourite wild mushroom. It grows in pinewoods on mountains all over the country. Bright saffron colour, it belongs to the milkcap family, but the drops it sheds when cut are red like blood. It is usually fried with parsley and garlic, and always expensive.

Rubio
The red gurnard. Good grilled and better baked with a sauce, as it can be dry.

S

Sábalo
Shad, a freshwater fish. Often served as ESCABECHE as it deteriorates fast once caught. It is also fried and served in a variety of sauces.

Sal
Salt; *salado* is salted. Fish are baked whole in salt, which is broken open, then discarded at table; see DORADA A LA SAL.

Salazón, en
Cured, that is, salted meat or fish.

◆◆ Salchichas
Fresh sausages. Excellent braised in sherry.

◆◆ Salchichón
A good, cured, ready-to-eat sausage – like a salami. *Salchichón de Málaga* has whole peppercorns in it.

Salema
One of the breams (fish); see DENTÓN.

Salmón
Salmon. They are caught in the north of the country. Steaks (*toros*) are grilled, while *arroz con salmón* is a good rice dish.

◆◆ Salmón a la gallega
Galician salmon. Cooked in stock and AGUARDIENTE, then served cold.

◆◆ Salmón a la ribereña
'River' salmon steaks, fried with raw ham, then served in a simple cider sauce.

Salmón ahumado
Smoked salmon.

◆◆ Salmonete
'Little salmon' are red mullet. Splendid grilled whole *a la parilla*. Tiny ones are fried and have the most beautiful flavour.

◆◆ Salmorejo, en
From 'cold set', this has become a word for game terrines; for example *perdices en salmorejo* are potted partridges.

◆◆◆ Salmorejo cordobés
Wonderful version of chilled GAZPACHO. A cream of garlic bread, tomatoes and oil, beaten to a light emulsion, with ham and chopped hard-boiled eggs. But beware! Sometimes it consists of just garlic, vinegar, oil and puréed bread.

Salmuera, en
In brine.

Salones
Literally 'salted', this may be cured lamb, kid or beef. The *salazones* of Valencia are salted, wind-dried fish, such as BONITO.

◆◆ Salpicón de mariscos
A shellfish 'cocktail' or salad; the French term means 'chopped' ingredients bound together in sauce. It can also be made with chicken (*de pollo*).

Salsa
Sauce. *Salsa de tomate* includes ketchup as well as tomatoes.

Salteado
Sautéed.

Salvia
Sage.

Sama de pluma
A bream (fish); see DENTÓN.

◆◆◆ Samfaina
One of the great Catalan sauces, and also a vegetable dish in its own right. It is made from aubergines, courgettes and peppers in an onion and tomato sauce. Chicken, pork and BACALAO are all cooked in it.

◆◆ San Jacobo
An international steak: beef fillet covered with ham and cheese.

◆ San Pedro
St Peter's fish has a black fingerprint on either side of its big head and is extremely tasty, with four big, bone-free fillets. It is also called *pez de John Dory* and cooked the same way as LUBINA.

◆◆ San Simón, queso de
A famous cows' milk cheese in Galicia, now factory made. It is smoked and looks like a well-oiled brown pear.

◆◆◆ Sancocho canario
A fish stew, best made of DENTÓN with potatoes. In the Canary Isles, it is served with a powerful red sauce that includes chillies and vinegar.

Sandía
Water melon.

◆ Santiaguiño
The flat clawless Galician lobster. It has the cross of St James on its head, hence the name. It is also called a *cigarra*

Sardines are caught off Cantábrica

Serrano *is eaten thinly sliced*

de mer (sea cricket) because it clicks in the water.

◆◆ Sardinas
Sardines. They are lovely barbecued simply on the beach. *A la santanderina* they are casseroled in tomato sauce.

Sargo
A bream. Good grilled or baked; see DENTÓN.

Sarten, de
'From the frying pan', as in *dulce de sarten* (deep-fried sweet pastries).

Seco
Dry or dried.

Sepia
Cuttlefish. Like purse-shaped squid; their flesh is sweeter but tougher. Small ones are grilled, but they are usually chopped and braised. The black ink from inside them – the original sepia ink – is used to finish the sauce; see ARRÓS NEGRE and CHIPIRONES.

◆◆ Sepia con guisantes
A pleasant stew of cuttlefish with peas.

◆ Sequillos
Hazelnut meringues.

◆◆◆ Serrano, jamón
The name means 'mountain-ham', usually called simply *serrano*. Eaten thinly sliced and raw on bread, as a *tapa*, or chopped for cooking. The best ham is *pata negra*, from black pigs running wild, and recognisable by the black toes of the trotter. The king of hams comes from Jabugo, north of Huelva. Others are made at Trevélez (less salty) and Montánchez. Less expensive (and leaner) hams are made from the white pig, and also from the shoulder (so not strictly ham). An amazing number of dishes include ham or ham stock.

Sesos
Brains. These are often included with other meats. *Sesos huecos* – nicknamed 'scatterbrains' – are creamy light fritters.

◆◆◆ Setas
A general term for all wild mushrooms. They are usually fried simply with garlic and parsley, occasionally with ham. They are also often served with eggs and as part of a game dish.

◆◆ Setas a la llauna
Wild mushrooms baked 'in a metal dish' in the oven with pork fat and garlic, in Catalunya.

Sidra, a la
Cooked in cider. Many fish are cooked this way on the north

coast, often with potatoes, which are fried first, then soaked in the sauce.

◆◆ Sobrasada
A soft, raw, red pork sausage, flavoured with paprika and with a great deal of fat. It is often served in pots, without the sausage casing, and is popular in Mallorca.

Sofrito
Onions fried slowly with garlic and parsley. This is a basic of Spanish cooking; tomato is usually added to make a sauce. The adjective means 'lightly fried'.

◆◆ Soldaditos de Pavía
The original fish finger. The Spanish equivalent of bread-and-butter 'soldiers', they are fried hake or BACALAO and commemorate the 'soldiers of General Pavía', who overthrew the first republic in 1874.

Solla
Not sole but plaice. Cooked like LENGUADO.

Solomillo
Beef fillet steak, from inside the sirloin bone. It may be roasted whole and served with fried onion rings.

Solomillo andaluz
Pork tenderloin – ie an economy version. *A la Trianera* (named after the Cádiz gypsy quarter) – roasted in sherry.

Sopa
Soup, made of the basic vegetables like *cebolla* (onion) as well as with rice (*sopa de arroz*) and pasta (*de fideos*). *Verduras* usually includes dried beans.

◆◆ Sopa AB or de vino
Named after the *amontillado* sherry from Gonzales Byass used in it.

◆◆ Sopa aragonesa
Made of minced calf's liver, grated cheese and broth, it is finished in the oven with a crust of bread and cheese.

◆◆ Sopa castellana
Garlic soup with cumin from La Mancha.

◆◆◆ Sopa de ajo
Basically this is water thickened with bread and flavoured with garlic: it can be appalling, but has many admirers. In Avila the bread for the *sopa de pobre* (for 'the poor') is fried first. In Rioja or Castile, it may have eggs beaten into it, and paprika for colour. Elsewhere it may contain poached eggs. The *sopa de gato*, cat soup in Cádiz, has grated cheese, and in Aragón garlic soup has lots of lemon.

◆◆ Sopa de albóndigas
Chicken broth with veal and ham meatballs, flavoured with cinnamon.

◆◆ Sopa de almendras
A sweet of almonds and bread, flavoured with cinnamon and lemon zest.

◆◆ Sopa de cangrejos
Delicious crab bisque, made in Mallorca.

◆◆◆ Sopa de mariscos or de pescados
Shellfish soup and fish soup. Often interchangeable: both contain both. Sometimes one fish is singled out, as in *sopa de gambas* (prawn soup); *sopa de pescadilla* (silver hake) or *sopa de rape* (monkfish). If you can afford it, *sopa de langosta* is lobster (crawfish) soup.

◆◆ Sopa de mejillones
Mussel soup. Good in Catalunya, with tomato, garlic and AGUARDIENTE.

◆◆ **Sopa de picadillo**
The name means soup with a
'chopped garnish' of ham,
hard-boiled eggs and fresh mint
– the latter as a hangover cure.
There are many egg and ham
soups, like *sopa alpurrañas*.

◆◆ **Sopa de tomate**
A soup with a long history in
Cádiz, made with tomatoes and
red peppers.

◆◆ **Sopa del cuarto de hora**
This '15-minute' soup – quick
compared to a broth – contains
fried onions and rice. It may
have prawns and chopped ham
and hard-boiled eggs in it. In
Cádiz, it may contain
Portuguese oysters.

◆◆ **Sopa mahimones,
maimones**
An Arab garlic, bread and olive
oil soup, possibly with ham. It is
finished in the oven to poach the
egg in it. Very hot and strong, it
is especially good when you are
tired and broke!

◆ **Sopa mallorquina**
Contains tomatoes, onions and
peppers, but is made very solid
with bread and not much liquid.

◆◆ **Sopas cachorreñas**
A fish soup flavoured with
pounded bitter orange zest,
vinegar and oil.

Soplillos
Fried sweet puffs with *anís* or
meringues with toasted
almonds.

Sospiros de Moros
Big puffy dry meringues in
Granada.

Suflé
A soufflé. Usually less good in
Spain than in France.

Suizos, (bollos)
Breakfast rolls, slashed down
the middle and baked with
sugar or currants in the hollow.

The name means 'Swiss' – how
different from Swiss roll!

◆◆◆ **Suquet, susquet,
susquillo de pescador**
A Catalan soup-stew with many
sorts of fish and shellfish, laced
with brandy and based on
onions and tomatoes, probably
with potatoes. Some are
thickened with pounded
almonds.

Suspiros de monja
'Nun's sighs', a popular dessert
of soft meringues poached in
milk, then served with custard.
Known as *oeufs à la neige* in
Britain and France and 'floating
islands' in the United States.
Suspiros are usually dry
meringues.

T

Tapa, tapaplana
Beef lower rump

Tarrina, en
Little brown earthenware pots
are used for CUAJADA and soft
cheese – the Spanish equivalent
of French white ramekins.

Tarta
Usually a cake or sweet pastry.
Tartita is any small dessert,
including ice-creams in pots.

◆ **Tarta de almendras**
Almond cake, often just ground
almonds, egg yolks and sugar,
like that from Puentedeume in
Galicia.

Tarta de manzana
Apple tart, often on puff pastry.

◆◆ **Tarta de Santiago**
In Santiago de Compostela on St
James's Day, this is a pastry tart
enclosing a moist almond filling.
The topping is decorated with a
stencil of St James's sword. In

Madrid, however, they dispense with the pastry and consequently it is a rather drier ground almond cake.

◆◆ Tarta helada
An ice-cream layer cake. *Tarta al whisky* has two different vanilla ice-creams, a whisky sponge layer and caramelised sugar on top.

Tarta Pasiega
A cheesecake, of fresh cheese of the type made in the Basque region, often flavoured with *anís*.

◆ Tejas
'Tiles'. Thin biscuits of egg white, ground almonds and sugar, like the French *tuiles*.

Tenca
Tench, a freshwater fish. Good marinated then fried or as ESCABECHE.

◆◆◆ Ternasco asado
Baby lamb, roast with white wine and lemon, a speciality in Aragón and Navarra.

Ternera
Often translated as 'veal', this is

Local dishes are usually available in smart restaurants

nearer to being virgin beef, as it can be up to two years old. *Ternera mechada* is 'larded', for a pot-roast or roast – good with *castañas* (chestnuts).

◆◆ Ternera a la sevillana
Veal cooked in Montilla wine, with olives.

◆◆ Ternera con alcachofas
Veal escalopes and artichoke bases in a sherry or tomato sauce.

Terrina
Cold terrine or pâté.

◆ Tetilla, queso de
A breast-shaped, soft white cows' milk cheese, now factory made in Galicia.

Tirabeques
Mangetout peas.

Tocino
Pork fat, fresh or salted, cut from the belly, and almost solid fat, even though it is the same cut as streaky bacon. It is cubed and fried to make a fine-

flavoured fat for cooking (and crisp bits) used in bean dishes. Sometimes *tocino* is fried bacon.

◆◆◆ Tocino de cielo
A dessert of pure sweetness and wonderful texture, it is served in small squares. Made from syrup and egg yolks, the name means 'heavenly bacon', because it looks like a bacon slab, as the sugar caramelises on top.

Tojunto
'All together'; *todo junto* is a one-pot mix of vegetables, rabbit and meat.

◆◆ Tomates rellenos
Stuffed tomatoes. In Alicante, spinach, nuts and orange are used.

Tomillo, en
With thyme, a popular herb.

Torradas
Fried TORRIJA, incorporated into a sweet omelette or custard.

Torrados
Toasted chick-peas.

Torreznos
Crisp, thick strips of fried pork belly.

◆ Torrija
A children's dessert of bread dipped in milk then fried and sugared. Like French *pain perdu*, it is made to use up stale bread.

Torta
A flat bun or a round or oval breakfast bread topped with crunchy sugar. It can also be a tart or a cake.

Torta de aceite
Plain pastry biscuits, made with oil.

◆◆ Torta del Casar
You are in luck if you find this rich, aromatic Extremeño ewes' milk cheese.

Tortas de hojaldre
Cake consisting of puff pastry layers with jam.

Tortells
A breakfast bread ring with a ground almond and lemon filling – and potato too – though you can't taste it.

◆◆◆ Tortilla española
A golden egg and potato cake, about the thickness of a sponge layer and shaped like it, this is *the* Spanish omelette. Delicious

---

Tortilla: True Spanish Omelette

There are many variations on the classic *tortilla española*, for example *espinacas* is with spinach and *gambas* is with prawns. *Tortilla hormigos o formigos* 'with ants' has crispy MIGAS (fried breadcrumbs) in it. A plain omelette is a *tortilla francesa*.

◆◆ **Tortilla a la catalana** is an omelette with beans and BUTIFARRA sausage.

◆◆ **Tortilla de Tudela** or **espárragos** is asparagus omelette.

◆◆ **Tortilla gallega** is an omelette with CHORIZO sausage and peppers.

◆ **Tortilla guisada** is served in tomato sauce.

◆ **Tortilla murciana** contains tomato and red peppers.

◆◆ **Tortilla paisana** often has a mixture of CHORIZO, potatoes, peppers, tomatoes, the lot!

◆◆◆ **Tortilla Sacramonte** is a famous (or infamous) gypsy omelette from Granada, with soft, smooth, white lambs' brains and (nowadays) sweetbreads, crisp MIGAS, peppers and potatoes.

when well made, eaten hot,
warm or cold, and popular as a
picnic filling in rolls. Wedges
are speared on sticks as *tapas*.

◆◆ Tortillitas de berenjenas
Aubergine fritters.

Tostadas
Literally 'toast'. Bread only very
lightly grilled to freshen it, and
used to mop up sauces.
Alternatively, it can be fried.

◆ Tostadas de crema
Not toast, but breakfast fingers
of cold custard, egged and
breadcrumbed, then fried.

◆◆◆ Tostón
Roast suckling pig.

Toyina
Salted tuna.

Trigo
Whole wheat, soaked. A *guiso
de trigo* or *triguillo* is a soup
with turnips and ACELGA stalks
or squash. *Olla de trigo* contains
chick-peas flavoured with
CHORIZO, bacon and chilli.

Trixat
Spanish bubble and squeak.
Cooked potato and cabbage,
plus chopped bacon, are
pressed into a mould, then fried
as a cake in pork fat.

Truchas
Trout. Brown trout still swim in
the fast streams of the Pyrenees
and Asturias, though restaurant
ones are likely to be farmed
and pink. Usually fried, but
good ESCABECHE.

◆◆ Truchas a la montañesa
Cantabrican trout cooked with
white wine, onion and bay
leaves. There is also a red wine
version (*en vino tinto*) in
Navarra.

◆◆ Truchas almendras
Trout fried and served with
fried almonds or *con salsa de
almendras*, usually a ground
almond sauce.

◆◆◆ Truchas con jamón
Ham slices are fried, then trout
are fried in the ham fat and
served stuffed or wrapped in
ham. This is also called *truchas
a la navarra*.

Trufa
Truffle. Found all over Spain but

A well stocked market stall

chiefly near Castellón de la Plana on the east coast.

Truita
Catalan for TORTILLA.

Trumfes
Catalan for potatoes.

Trumfes fadrines
Potatoes 'on their own', served with a little ham and egg-thickened sauce added at the last minute.

◆ **Ttoro, tioro**
A Basque mixed fish stew or soup, with onion, bread and wine.

Tuétano
Bone marrow. Usually grilled slices.

◆ **Tumbet, tombet**
A vegetable stew from Mallorca, with tomatoes and aubergine, like *ratatouille* with potatoes added. It can be rather oily. Sometimes it is layered with meat or contains eggs, and there are also fish versions.

◆◆◆ **Turrón**
A candy-like Italian *nougat*. *Jijona blando* is a soft coffee-coloured paste of ground toasted almonds and honey. Alicante *turrón* is white and hard, studded with whole nuts.

Tx
The Basque for CH, which is how it is pronounced; see CH.

Txangurro, changurro
The Basque word for a spider crab; see CENTOLLO.

U

◆◆◆ **Urta a la roteña**
A bream, related to DENTÓN. Found on the southwest coast, it feeds on shellfish and so tastes

of them. It is cooked in a naturally-sweet sauce made by frying onions until they caramelise, then adding tomato which is reduced very slowly.

Uvas
Grapes.

V

Vaca
Cow, giving beef and milk for *queso de vaca*, cheese.

Venado
Venison. A coarse meat, it is often stewed with thyme.

◆◆◆ **Venado con cabrales**
The best cuts of venison roasted and with a blue cheese sauce.

Veneras
Scallops.

Verduras
Green vegetables. Often a separate course, or included in rice or MENESTRA.

Vieiras
The Galician name for scallops.

◆◆ **Vieiras al alberiño**
Scallops cooked in the local white wine.

◆◆◆ **Vieiras de Santiago** or **Santiagüenses**
Scallops in Santiago de Compostela are flamed in brandy, arranged in the upper curved shell with tomato sauce and topped with breadcrumbs, then quickly grilled.

◆ **Vieja**
The colourful 'widow' fish, purple backed and yellow finned, is very typical of the Canary Isles. It has very delicate flesh, which is poached with potatoes.

◆ **Villalón, queso de**
A soft rectangular ewes' milk

cheese in Castile, sometimes shaped like a hoof.

◆◆ Villeroy
A French dish, popular in Spain, of chicken breasts or prawns coated in béchamel, chilled then crumbed. They are fried and served hot.

Vinagre
Vinegar. The best, *jerez*, is made from sherry.

Vinagreta
Vinaigrette.

Viuda
'Widowed'. The word can apply to a meatless POTAJE and to PATATAS – and also to small, grey snails.

Vizcaina
The Spanish word for Biscay. *Salsa a la vizcaina* includes onions and dried peppers, but not tomato.

X

◆◆ Xató, xatonada
Mixed dressed salad from Tarragona containing salted cod, sometimes tuna and anchovy fillets too, and often tomato and olives.

Xuxos
Fried doughnuts. Nowadays served with whipped cream, originally fried round a stick, then custard-filled.

Y

◆◆ Yemas
Very sweet, small, yellow cakes. Named after the egg yolks used to make them and which they resemble. Nuns make these candies by combining egg yolks with boiling syrup. The egg paste is then moulded into 'yolk' shapes, sugared and left to dry. *Yemas de San Leandro* in Seville and those of *Santa Teresa* in Avila are celebrated.

Z

Zamorana, a la
Dishes from Zamora. These often include black MORCILLA, onion and paprika.

Zapata, zapatero
Means a 'shoe', but this is a fish of the bream family; see DENTÓN.

◆ Zarangollo
A hash of onion and courgettes, well-garlicked, and served with fried bread.

Zarzamoras
Blackberries.

◆◆◆ Zarzuela
Given the name 'light opera', this dish is a wonderful medley of white fish with a display of shellfish in a tomato, wine and saffron broth. A culinary star on the Catalan coast.

Zizak
Basque for St George's mushroom; see MOIXERNON.

Zoque
Chilled, strained, vinegared, raw tomato and pepper soup, much like GAZPACHO. Served over bread or TOSTADAS.

Zorza
Fried pork with paprika, like skinless CHORIZO.

Zurrón
Means a knapsack, or a small game bag, so in culinary terms something stuffed, such as small birds inside peppers.

WINES OF SPAIN

Vineyards cover a huge area of Spain; but even the famous ones may look scrubby and ill-kempt to those familiar with well-ordered French or German vines. A vast amount of wine is produced. It is high-alcohol stuff, often over 12 per cent, and most of it is drunk young. Spaniards have never made a fetish of matching 'appropriate' wines with food. And nowadays even the connection between regional food and regional wine hardly exists. This is because the Spanish wine industry has been ruthlessly restructured on commercial lines. The new wines, however, are of a type tourists are likely to enjoy, because they are mainly based on French models.

When the *phylloxera* louse devastated the French vineyards in the 1860s, French wine-makers moved south. They settled in the two areas which are now famous for quality wine in Spain: Rioja and Penedès. Here they introduced French methods of viniculture and even French grapes, so bottles from these two areas contain the better wines on a wine list. Restructuring did not stop there. In the 1970s the sherry houses, in particular those which already had efficient export businesses, became involved in making red and white wine. They researched international markets, particularly the United States, and started producing wines to suit those palates. The Spanish liked the new wines, too, and they are now widely sold inside Spain.

*In the following text the denominated wine areas, **DO**, are given in bold.*

Young wines

At home, Spaniards prefer to drink uncomplicated *vino corriente*. This is table wine, sold the first or second year after harvesting. These young reds are free of tannin, which would make ageing possible, so they taste fresh and fruity. As a result, they make remarkably pleasant – and pleasantly cheap – drinking. Even in Rioja, Spain's most famous wine area, only 40 per cent of the wine is aged in barrels.

The biggest BODEGA in Rioja is Campo Viejo, and their best seller in Spain is San Ascensio *2° año sin crianza* wine, which means 'sold in the second year after harvest, without wood ageing'. Another household brand of young red Rioja – Ernest Hemingway's favourite – is Banda Azul *3° año*, from Frederick Paternina, the country's largest exporter. The *3° año* from CUNE, another major firm, is also popular.

WINE REGIONS

Rioja

In Spain there is the welcome opportunity to drink quality wines at a lower cost than elsewhere in Europe. In the Ebro valley in northern Spain, Rioja is celebrated for medium reds. The characteristic that distinguishes them as Spanish wines is a distinct flavour of vanilla, which comes from storage in oak casks. They have a softer, less delicate, but fruitier taste than French wines

Vineyard near Tarragona

of equal quality. Rioja also makes respectable white wines. Rioja wines are produced by a few major companies these days and they are very definitely blended wines – some firms actually own no vineyards at all! They buy grapes and mix varieties, so you are buying blending skill and a brand name. The trick is to find a taste you like, then look for the houses that make it.

On the one hand, there are the traditional houses, which believe in maturing the wine in oak casks (see CRIANZA) until it absorbs a positive flavour of oak. Marqués de Murrieta is the most imposing of these, but others are Paternina, CUNE and Bodegas Riojanas. Some newer firms, like Muga, make quality wines the old way, too. The easiest to remember are the 'three mighty Ms' – Muga and the Marquéses of Murrieta and Riscal. The law specifies minimum periods in the barrel, but traditional houses may exceed this, and older wines are also likely to have a longer barrel age. La Rioja Alta's Viña Ardanza, for example, spends longer in the cask than in the bottle.

On the other hand, there are the modern *bodegas* that have gone for the minimum barrel ageing (see CRIANZA). They favour maturing in the bottle instead. The Marqués de Cáceres and Langunilla are in this camp, along with Olarro and Spain's third biggest exporter, Faustino Martínez (their labels have a face on them). The last two are popular in America.

Almost all white Rioja wine is made from the traditional Viura grape. White wine is also made in two different styles. The traditional way is to age it in oak, like red wine. Marqués de Murrieta is the most renowned white in this style. Try their RESERVA, which is lemony, but rich and buttery with the flavour of oak, or Monte Reál from Bodegas Riojanas or a white from López de Heredia. A new popular white is CUNE's Monopole *blanco*. This has only a modest amount of oakiness, and a freshness that is half way to the new style.

The new style whites are more like French wines and are made in vats. The results are crisper and fresher, with more fruit flavour. The best of these is Marqués de Cáceres, a 'poor man's Sancerre'.

Apart from the actual method of making wine, geography is an important factor in taste – the wine-makers have, after all, to get their grapes from somewhere. Written at the bottom of each wine label is the headquarters of the firm. Wines from the **Rioja Baja** (the lower southern end) are the fruitier, everyday wines. The cooler, higher end, the **Rioja Alta**, produces wines with the highest acidity. This means they are hard when young, but mature into something more complex. Rioja Alta RESERVAS are likely to be smooth, firm and of a high quality.

There is a third Rioja district called the **Rioja Alavesa**, which is made up of parcels of land on the north side of Rioja Alta. The wines from here are softer, more aromatic and sometimes fuller-bodied.

Navarra and Aragón

Navarra is the district adjoining Rioja, and its wines share many characteristics with those of Rioja. Well balanced reds are made in the Ribera Alta and lighter ones in Valdizarbe.

Young Navarra reds are rather like *Beaujolais nouveau*. Chivite is the name to look for. Navarra also makes the best-finished ROSADOS in Spain: try Gran Feudo.

In **Aragón**, hefty purplish-coloured reds, often 15 per cent or more alcohol, are made in **Cariñena**; they have slightly more balancing acidity than the dull reds from the south. **Borja** reds are similar, with strong ROSADOS, but in **Somontano** the reds are lighter.

Northeast Coast

The main difference between **Penedès** and Rioja (the two quality wine areas) is that Rioja is famed for wine aged in oak, but Penedès chose the French style of bottle ageing instead – and introduced French grapes. Penedès is predominantly a white wine region, with good vines growing in the cooler hills. It is one of the main areas of experiment in Spain, the best wines being made from acclimatised foreign grapes, or from these mixed with Spanish grapes.

The big producer here is Torres. Their easy summer white wine Viña Sol – fresh, dry and a bit lemony – is made exclusively from Parellada, the Spanish grape, though in the French style. Torres Gran Viña Sol has a slight pineapple taste because it is half made from Chardonnay grapes, while the rich white and much grander Gran Viña Sol 'Green Label', made with some Sauvignon grapes, is unusual both in being estate-bottled (at Castell de Fransola) and as one of the few

white wines matured in oak.
Far less red wine is made. Gran
Sangre de Toro, deep red and
fruity, is one of the few still
typical of wine produced in the
region in times past. Torres
Gran Coronas, however, is more
than half Cabernet Sauvignon,
which gives it body and
fruitiness, while the luscious –
and expensive – 'Black Label' is
all Cabernet Sauvignon.
Another experimental (and tiny)
firm is owned by American Jean
León, who specialises in classic
imported vine varieties. Raimat,
in the **Costers de Segre**, is
known for quality wines, one
being a Cabernet Sauvignon.
Raimat Abadia also includes the
Cabernet Sauvignon grape.
Raimat also makes a rich
buttery-tasting white from
another grape new to Spain,
Chardonnay. There are also
some luscious Chardonnay
cavas (see page 82).
Firms like Masia Bach
specialise in old indigenous
vine varieties. This company
makes one of the very few fresh
but sweet Spanish white wines
(see **Dessert Wines**, page 82).
Alella is the second major wine
area in Catalunya, and its whites
are popular in Barcelona, for the
district is just north of the city.
Marqués de Alella makes
delicate young white wines,
with a prickly edge. **Tarragona**
is also white wine country, and
famed for dessert wines (see
page 82) – and for making
communion wines.
The best red – powerful, classic
and full-bodied – comes from
Priorato. Look for labels with
angels on ladders or 'Scala Dei'.
The **Ampurdán** makes good

*Valdepeñas red wines are fermented
in amphora-like jars*

cherry-coloured ROSADOS – and
the light red VI NOVELL.

La Mancha and Valdepeñas
It takes hours and hours to drive
across the great plains of **La
Mancha**, a vast area containing
half Spain's vineyards. The wine
is rough – and deep-yellow not
white – and made from the
Airén grape. However, a few
(rather bland) bottles are
blended for export.
Valdepeñas is a small wine area
in the south almost enclosed by
the larger La Mancha district.
Here better quality wine is
made and the huge *tinajas*, or
Ali Baba wine jars, that stand by
the roadside are actually used
in the wine-making process.
Traditionally, Valdepeñas is
famous for ALOQUES: strong but
light red wines, made from a
blend of red and white grapes.
Now the better reds are made
with fruity Cenibel, the best red
Rioja grape (check on the

WINES OF SPAIN

label), and there are some oak-aged wines at Señoria de Los Llanos. Near **Toledo** the Marqués de Griñon makes fine Cabernet Sauvignon wines.

Levante and the Southeast

The hot plains and hills of the southeast are Spain's largest producers of red wine: high-alcohol reds, with no acidity, which makes them taste very dull. **Alicante** reds are typical, though **Utiel-Requena** makes a lighter and more acid red and the area's best, most fragrant light ROSADA.

Jumilla produces dark, full-bodied and lethal reds, with an alcohol content of up to 18 per cent – just the thing if you want to have a big meal and get rather drunk as well! SAVIN, Spain's biggest wine company, has a huge plant here, making a rather lighter and fresher *tinto*. Red **Yecla** is bigger-bodied, though a bit lower in alcohol. **Valencia** is Spain's chief wine port, and its local wine is white, the best being from Alto Turia. However, if you want a refreshing, fruity local wine anywhere in southeast Spain, a good bet might be ROSADO, as many good rosés are made here.

The Southwest

Many Spanish white wines taste remarkably like sherry. The hot sun produces sugar in the grape, which turns into dry alcohol. These wines may come as a surprise if you are not expecting them – but in Spain sherry is often the wine drunk with fish anyway. The white wines of **Extremadura** (try Cañamero and Chiclana, which

is the white of Cádiz), fall into this category.

The best known of these wines, however, comes from sherry's neighbouring district – **Montilla-Moriles** – and *amontillado* is derived from the town's name. There, high alcohol levels are achieved without fortifying the wine, though fortified wines are also made. One of the best known *finos* in the south is Alvear's CB, and therefore is not in fact a sherry.

The **Condado de Huelva** is known for wines like sherry and GENEROSO, but increasingly it produces white table wines.

The Northwest and Central North

The cooler, wetter north of Spain is celebrated for fresh white wines, made in traditional ways from traditional Spanish grapes. In the Basque country they make TXACOLI on the sea coast: the white tastes of apples, is rather acid, and slightly *pétillant*.

In Galicia, there is also a small class of 'green' wines. Made in **Ribeiro** and the **Rias Baixas**, they differ from other wines in Spain in being more like German wines. Here the ALBARIÑO grape makes delicately fruity wines, which prickle slightly in the mouth: some of Spain's best shellfish wines.

The red wine most drunk in Galicia is the fruity, light-coloured **El Bierzo**, from the south of the province. In Old Castile, **León** makes some good oak-aged reds, especially from the Palacio de Arganza. Look

Southern wines in the wood

for the acronym VILE – they aren't vile at all! But avoid the black wines of Orense, which are. **Cigales**, long famous makes CLARETE by mixing black and white grapes.

Toro is reputedly the oldest red wine in Spain – although the newest *Denominación de Origen* (demarcated) district. It went with Columbus to America and is known as the 'thinking wine' of Salamanca University for its popularity with the students. Full-bodied with a hint of damson about it, the wine has a pleasantly lingering after-taste. Bodegas Fariña is the name to look for.

In the north of Old Castile, **Rueda** has had a boom in pleasant, fruity, young whites, which are not very alcoholic. It is a long-established white wine area, and they use the local and characterful Verdejo grape. Both Marqués de Griñon and Marqués de Riscal (which make red wines elsewhere – Riscal in Rioja) make their white wines

here, and they are some of the best in Spain.

Ribera del Duero, high up in the north of Old Castile, produces what is indisputably the most famous red wine in Spain, often 10 years in the barrel: Vega Sicilia. Smart restaurants buy up all their output. Younger, but still expensive, wines called Valbuena come from the same place. However, the local Ribera del Duero co-operative makes the affordable fruity Peñafiel wines. To the east, **Burgos** makes a light CLARETE.

SHERRY

Sherry is one of the world's great white wines, and it is certainly the cheapest of them. It comes from Jerez, one of the few areas in Spain with a wine tradition to boast about. It is mainly made from the Palomino grape and blended on a SOLERA system of stacked barrels in huge buildings likened to 'sherry cathedrals'.

Native grape varieties prevail in the production of Spanish wine

It is a fortified wine, and its high alcohol content has made it a before- or after-dinner wine, though in Spain *fino* is drunk as white wine.

Sherries are ranked for export by sweetness, though in Spain each category can vary quite widely. FINO and MANZANILLA are dry, AMONTILLADO is nutty and medium-dry, PALO CORTADO comes in sweetness between this and OLOROSO, which is a mature, and usually sweeter, sherry.

DESSERT WINES

Do not skip this part of the meal, even if you think you don't like sweet wine, for these are the true desserts of Spain.

Masia Bach's Extrésimo *blanco semi dulce* is rare in being both fresh-tasting yet honeyed, because most of Spain's other dessert wines are darker and much stronger.

Muscat is the main grape for dessert wines, often left to wrinkle and concentrate on the vine. In Alicante, the Roman Moscatel is one of the finest, while Moscatel de Valencia has a slight orange edge.

In the 18th century, **Málaga** *Dulce* was famous in Britain as 'Mountain Wine', and again in the 19th century in America. Drinking it is like sipping sultanas. It certainly makes a much nicer end to a meal than a bad ice-cream. Smooth LÁGRIMA is the sweetest, Málaga Virgin the best known. Or try Scholtz Hermanos Solera 1885, which has a walnut scent.

VI RANCIOS are made in Alicante and **Tarragona** in a SOLERA system, for they are fortified dessert wines. Tarragona also makes *clásicos*, sweet wines, both red and white, and over a fifth alcohol!

CAVAS

CAVAS are sparkling wines, made by the champagne method in **Penedès**, although the grapes may come from other DO *cava* areas. They mainly originate from San Sadurní de Nova where the big houses are based, including Codorníu, the largest champagne-style wine-maker in the world. Freixenet Cordon Negro (in a black bottle) is also popular. The Spanish like their *cavas* on the sweet side. If you do not, look for *brut* or *brut natur*. There are also lovely, but expensive, *champáns* made from Chardonnay grapes. The best is from Codorníu, but a good alternative comes from Raimat.

A-Z OF DRINKS

A

Abocado
Semi-sweet table wine.

Agua mineral
Mineral water. It is sold everywhere, sparkling, *con gas*, or flat, *sin gas*. Some of it is bottled at famous spas like Lanjarón.

Agua potable
Drinking water.

Aguardiente
Any distilled liquor. The clear, *anís*-flavoured one is a favourite. *Aguardiente de orujo* is a rough grape brandy, like *marc*.

Aguja
Slightly sparkling.

◆ Albariño
The famous 'green' wine of Galicia, flowery but somewhat acid. Good with shellfish. It is made close to the Portuguese *vinho verde* region and from the same grape. It has a slight fizz as well, though the famous one from Palacio de Fefiñanes is still. However, you will find them less sweet than *vinho verde*.

Aloque
Red wine made from white grapes mixed with only 10 per cent red ones. Light but surprisingly alcoholic wines.

◆◆◆ Amontillado
A famous style of sherry, amber-yellow, walnut flavoured and medium dry, though in Spain there are drier ones too. They are made from FINO, adding more wine spirit and maturing to become softer and darker. The best are old *finos* not suitable for drinking young.

Añejo
Old, mature or aged.

◆◆ Anís
One of Spain's favourite liqueurs, colourless, flavoured with aniseed and made all over the country. Much used for flavouring biscuits and desserts. There is dry (*seco*) drunk with water as an aperitif, and sweet (*dulce*).

Año
Means 'year' and many popular wines are sold the second or third year after harvest.

B

Bebidas
A general word for drinks. But under this name come a series of sweet fruit *eaux de vie*, often in frosted bottles, with names like *Bebidas de melecotón* (peach) and flavours like hazelnut. The Spanish also mix fruit syrups with gin 'on the rocks'. Rives make flavours like passion fruit, pomegranate and the green kiwi.

Blanco, vino
White wines. In Spain these come in more varieties than they do in France. Many of them taste like sherry, particularly from the hot southwest and west. Then there are the aristocratic traditional white ones, that are aged in oak barrels. French-style white wines are made too, which are much crisper, fresh and fruity. There are a very few sweet white wines, but more sparkling wines, called CAVAS, and many golden dessert wines, from grapes like Muscat or Malvasía.

◆ **Blanco y negro**
Iced milk and coffee, scented
with cinnamon.

Bodega
A wine store where wine and
sherry are made, and so the
company that makes the wine.
Brands are very important in
Spanish wine.

Brut, brut natur
Extra dry wine. This appears
only on sparkling wine.

C

Café
Coffee. Brewed dark and strong
in Spain. *Café solo* is black
coffee in tiny cups, while *un
corto* or *café cortado* is the
identical amount of coffee
served in a small tumbler with a
little milk. *Café con leche* will
be half milk to bring it to
breakfast strength.
Descafeinado is always instant
decaffeinated. However, if you
order iced coffee (*café helado*)
do not be surprised if a cup of
coffee arrives with a glass of ice
cubes. Pour the coffee on the
cubes – it cools instantly.

◆ **Carajillo, el**
A small black coffee with a shot
of brandy or *anís* in it. A Catalan
joke – the name means a 'willy'.

Castillo, castell
Château-bottled wines. There
are comparatively few of these
wines in Spain, which means all
the grapes come from the
estate. Good ones come from
Marqués de Murrieta at Castel
Ygay in Rioja, Torres Gran Viña
Sol 'Green Label' at Castell de
Fransola and Raimat in
Penedès.

◆◆ **Cavas**
Spanish sparkling wines, made
by the champagne method,
when they acquire their sparkle
in the bottle. Well worth trying if
you avoid the sweet ones!
Cordorníu is the world's largest
producer.

Cepa
Grape.

◆ **Cerveza**
Spanish lager. As it is good with
plenty of flavour, it is not worth
paying for *cerveza extranerja*
(imported beer). Try San
Miguel *especial*, Aguila, or
Victoria brands. Majou is the
best bitter and this is also less
gassy.

Champán
Champagne-style. *Champaña* is
French champagne.

◆ **Chocolate caliente**
Hot chocolate. Try it for
breakfast, with crusty rolls to
dip into it. The powder or
tablets are sold with a thickener
already added, and just need
hot milk.

Clarete
As well as *vino tinto*, a second
type of red wine is made, light
enough to drink without food.
Good ones are made in
Valdepeñas, by mixing black
and white grapes. Others are
made in El Bierzo and Cigales
in Old Castile, Valle de
Montessey in the northwest, and
Extremadura. They have no
connection with French claret.

◆◆ **Coñac**
Brandy. An extremely popular
after-dinner drink – and
policemen on early-morning
patrol have a shot with their
breakfast coffee. Some brandies
are smoother, in the French
fashion, while the roughish but

grapey Fundador is liked by foreigners. However, Spaniards favour caramelised brandies, which are sweeter and more perfumed. Veterano is one good brand and the smooth and aromatic Magno is popular.

Copitas

The tall, tulip-shaped glasses from which sherry is drunk. They narrow towards the top to hold the aroma.

Corriente, vino

A table wine sold the year of, or two years after, harvest. Most Spaniards drink this with their meals.

Cosecha

The year of the harvest, given on the bottle. Most Spanish wine is drunk young, but the ageing of wine is regulated in three classes, with a minimum number of years for each class. A wine that is old for its class may be a good one, but a red wine SIN CRIANZA, that is over three years, is a stale bottle not worth drinking.

Cremas

Sweet liqueurs. Ask *¿Es un licor?* if in doubt. The best known orange liqueur (*crema de naranja*) is Curaçao in various colours including blue (*azul*). Triple Sec, which is less sticky, is worth trying. Others are crème de menthe (*crema de menta*) and coffee and chocolate liqueurs (*crema de café y crema de cacao*).

◆◆ Cremat

A potent Costa Brava coffee including brandy and rum, which are first flamed.

Crianza

'Aged in wood'. It is this that gives Spanish wines, and Rioja in particular, their distinctive 'Spanish' taste. The barrels are made of oak, and new barrels make wine taste strongly of vanilla, so this is used, like spices in cooking, to flavour the wine.

The labelling laws specify how much time in the barrel each wine must have in each of three categories: *crianza*, RESERVA and GRAN RESERVA. All whites and ROSADOS have a minimum of six months, reds one year, and red *Gran reservas* a minimum of two years.

Bringing in the grape harvest

Some companies decide to exceed the minimums, as part of the house style, which is why some old-fashioned Riojas have a strong whiff of vanilla. Others take the opposite path. The wine-makers of Penedès decided to age most of their wines in bottles instead, which makes their wines taste more like French wines. The majority of Riojan white wines are now not barrel-aged at all.

Crianza, sin
Most ordinary wines come into this class stored in vats, not barrels.

Cubalibre
Rum and coke or, in Spain, frequently gin and coke.

D

DO, Denominación de Origen
Similar to French *appellation contrôlée*, a designated quality control area.

Dulce
Sweet.

E

Embotellado por
Bottled for.

Espumoso
Any sparkling wine.

F

◆◆◆ Fino
The best of the sherry styles, being dry, light and at around 17 per cent, the least alcoholic type. It is a blended wine, made in a SOLERA system. A small dose of alcoholic spirit is added to the young wine, which still allows a thick yeast, called *flor*, to develop on top. This protects the wine being oxidised by air above it. *Finos* are Spain's finest white wines and age well, but they also have qualities to make them perfect young.

G

Gaseoso
Fizzy drink.

◆ Generoso, un vino
A fortified wine, drunk before or after a meal. Look for Condado Viejo de Huelva. They are also made in Rueda and the Ampurdán.

Ginebra
Gin, made by the huge firm of Larios. It is often drunk short with ice and sweet mixers (see BEBIDAS) and with soda and lemon, *en pallofa*.

◆◆◆ Gran reserva
Much of Spain's best wine falls into this category and they are not expensive compared with matured French wines.
In exceptional years, the wine-makers will earmark the vintage for preferential treatment. A *Gran reserva* may not be sold until the sixth year after harvest, and a red wine must spend a minimum of two years ageing in oak casks. White wines must spend at least six months in the casks. They are then moved to bottles to finish maturing.

Granvas
A sparkling wine made in tanks and so less good than a CAVA.

H

Hielo, con
With ice or 'on the rocks'.
Holandas
Not gin, but grape spirit, distilled in the poorer parts of Spain and used to make sherry and brandy.
◆ **Horchata**
A creamy drink, sometimes iced, made from ground tiger nuts (see CHUFA in **A–Z of Foods**), sweetened with honey. It is sold freshly made in the south and Madrid.

I

◆ **Infusiones**
Herbal teas (also called *tisanas*) are very popular in Spain. Camomile is *manzanilla* (don't get it confused with the sherry), either bitter or sweet. Mint tea is *poleomenta, tila* is lime and *hierba luisa* is lemon verbena.

J

Jerez
Sherry – a mispronunciation of this place-name. Because it is a fortified wine, it is drunk as an aperitif outside Spain. But Spaniards think of FINO as a dry white wine. It should be drunk from a half bottle, kept on ice.
Jugo de fruta
Fruit juice. *Pomelo, limón* and *naranja* are grapefruit, lemon and orange. *Manzana* and *piña* are apple and pineapple.

Gin in a variety of shapes

L

◆ **Lágrima, vino de**
Wine from 'tears', ie juice from grapes that are so ripe that it drips without crushing. As a result the wines are old-gold, with a luscious sweet finish.
Leche
Milk. This is safe but homogenised, in UHT packs, so not particularly attractive to drink. One big firm, Puleva, also sells pasteurised milk in glass bottles, which makes a better cup of British tea. Flavoured milk is *un batido*.
◆ **Leche meringuada**
A summer drink, and sometimes an ice, of milk with sweet meringue in it.

A–Z OF DRINKS

◆ Licor

Liqueur. They take the place of desserts to make a sweet finish to the meal. Two popular ones are the Catalan Calisay, a quinine-based, herbal liqueur with a sweetish aftertaste – good 'on the rocks'. Licor 43 (Cuarenta y tres) is clear orange in colour, vanilla flavoured and sweet, with a lingering finish.

Limonada

Sweet fizzy lemonade. Popular brands are Fanta, in one-person cans, and La Casera, a slightly lemony-tasting soda, used for diluting drinks.

M

Malvasía

A sweet dessert wine which takes its name from the grape that also makes Malmsey.

◆◆◆ Manzanilla

The driest and most delicate of pale-gold sherries. The taste comes from storing chosen light FINO sherries at Sanlúcar de Barrameda by the sea, where they pick up that faint salty tang. It has taken the name of camomile.

Manzanilla

Camomile. A popular herbal tea.

Mistela

Grape juice mixed with wine alcohol: an aperitif.

◆◆ Moscatel

The muscat grape gives its name to many sweet wines. In the south and Valencia, they are famous for their sultana taste, though the old ones often taste like toffee too. The best come from Málaga, though they are also made in Asturias and Penedès. For more information see page 82.

O

◆ Oloroso

A dark golden and the most full-bodied type of sherry. It is usually sweet and at least 18 per cent alcohol. All sherry starts off dry and develops in contact with the air – unlike wine. Olorosos are developed in a different SOLERA from FINOS. The new wine is fortified with more spirit at the beginning, and no yeast will grow on this. Olorosos mature by gradually oxidising. Good olorosos are reminiscent of port, though, there are dryer ones. 'Cream' sherry is made by adding juice from the Pedro Ximénez grape.

P

◆ Pacharán

The top generic liqueur in Spain. Made from sloes, red or brown, sweet and anís-flavoured, it is well worth trying 'on the rocks' before and after meals. Zoco is the best known brand.

◆◆ Palo cortado

A rarer type of sherry because it occurs by accident. It is darker than AMONTILLADO and in sweetness comes between it and OLOROSO.

◆ Pedro Ximénez

One of the sherry grapes, all of which start dry. But it is also used for luscious dessert wines and its juice is added to

OLOROSOS, to make a 'cream' sherry.

◆ Ponche

In a silver bottle will be a herbalised old brandy: sweeter than ordinary brandy but less sticky than a liqueur. De Soto has a faint taste of orange. *Ponche* means 'punch' and includes drinks such as hot milk whisked with brandy and egg yolks.

Porrón

A wine bottle with a long spout for communal drinking without touching the mouthpiece.

◆ Punys d'ous

Menorca milk punch, which also contains rum, lemons, eggs and sugar.

Q

◆◆◆ Queimada

A powerful drink said to need three men – two to hold up the man who drinks it! Making it is a magic ritual in Galicia, where AGUARDIENTE DE ORUJO is poured in a bowl with sugar and apple slices or coffee beans and then flamed. Drinking starts when the flames die down.

R

◆ Rancio, vi (vino)

This mellowed dessert wine is fortified then aged in contact with the air, either in glass jars, left in the sun, or in a SOLERA of oak casks. The 20-year-old Fondillón is famous.

Refrescos

'Cool' drinks implying soft ones.

◆◆ Reserva

These are the wines you are most likely to find back home – of reasonable quality, with some ageing. They are wines sold four years after harvest. Whites and ROSADOS have spent at least six months in oak casks, and reds at least a year, often much more. The result is a well balanced wine, with a satisfying aftertaste. *Reservas* include both modest wines labelled only with the region, like a Navarra, and branded wines from companies in good areas like Rioja and Penedès.

Ron

Rum. Spain grows sugar cane and makes rum, dark rum and the famous colourless Bacardi (under licence), drunk simply with lemon juice and ice or as a CUBALIBRE, with coke.

◆ Rosado

Rosé wine. The ones from Navarra are well finished and *rosés* are also made in Aragón and Ribera del Duero. On the southeast coast, where the red wine is soupy and very alcoholic, they are a good buy. Try the one made in Tarragona or the cherry-coloured *rosado* from Ampurdán. Utiel-Requena makes pale, refreshing ones.

S

◆◆◆ Sangría

The celebrated chilled wine punch dilutes the southern red wine, which is very high in alcohol, with citrus juice, ice and cold water – and adds a kick again with brandy. (See recipe page 113.)

A–Z OF DRINKS

Seco
Dry.

◆ Sidra
Cider. Very popular in the Basque country, where *sidrerías* (cider shops) offer drink and food. Much drunk in Asturias.

Sifón
Soda water.

◆ Sol y sombra
'Sun and shade' is a hefty drink of sweet dark brandy, with a slug of *anís*.

Solera
The system in which sherries are blended. The name refers to a stack of barrels, often five rows high. New wine is first sorted by style – either a FINO or OLOROSO type. It is then put into the topmost barrel of a *solera* of the same group. As wine is taken from the older barrels, so they are each topped up from barrels of younger wine.

Fino wine for sampling is drawn from the bottom row, by a little cup on a long stem, called a *venencia*, and then thrown in a great arc into a glass. The best and most expensive sherries come direct from the *solera*, without further blending.

T

Té con leche
Tea with milk. *Con limón* is with lemon. Iced tea is *té helado*.

Tinto, vino
Red wine. Usually a better bet in Spain.

◆ Txacoli, chacoli
The Basques are proud of this thin, rather acidic, white wine from vineyards by the sea. It has a faint taste of apples.

V

◆ Verde, vino
'Green wines'. These are the fresh whites of Galicia.

Vermú
Vermouth. A dry one with ice is *vermú blanco seco con hielo*, a popular lunchtime drink in Spain.

Vi novell
New wine. Modelled on *Beaujolais nouveau*, in Ampurdán.

Vino
Wine, pronounced with a soft B – 'bino'. A *viña* is a vineyard, while *vino de paso* is homemade raisin wine.

Vino de meso, de pasto
Table wine.

Vino de Oporto
Port.

Vodka
Just as it looks. With tonic is *y tónic*.

W

Whisky americano
Bourbon.

Whisky sifón
Pronounced 'whicky', with soda.

Z

Zumo de naranja natural
Freshly squeezed orange juice.

◆ Zurracapote
A hot red Rioja punch with cinnamon and brandy.

◆ Zurro
A white wine cooler from La Mancha.

SHOPPING

In this and later chapters, words and phrases are included to help you deal with everyday situations. Phonetic pronunciation guides are given, but for more information on pronouncing Spanish see **Language** page 125.

TYPES OF SHOPS

Supermarkets have come to Spain in a big way, but you will also find corner stores, specialist food shops and lots of street markets. If you can find one of the latter, or if you go to a *Hiper* or a *Pryca* (vast supermarkets) early in your visit, bulk shopping will save you a lot of money.
Equally, don't be embarrassed about buying in very small quantities. Spanish people point and often buy 100g (¼lb) at a time.
Un almacén is a big store, *una tienda de comestibles* a food shop and *una mantequería* is a general grocery. *La panadería* sells only bread, but in *una pastelería* you can get sweet breakfast rolls as well as cakes and biscuits. Your children may pester you to stop at *una bombonería*, sweet stall.

BASIC STORES

You will find most of the items you buy at home in Spanish supermarkets – with small differences. For instance, canned tomato comes in three convenient ways. *Tomato pelado* are whole tomatoes, while *tomate triturado* is minced and *tomato frito* is a thick tomato sauce, which drowns everything if you use too much. And don't

Delicatessen and bar combined

Going Shopping

Is there a supermarket near here?
  ¿Hay un supermercado por aquí?
  A-ee oon soo-per-mer-kA-do por a-Kee

What day is the market?
  ¿Qué días hay mercado?
  ke dEE-as a-ee mer-kA-do

I want (need) to buy . . .
  Quiero comprar . . .
  kyEh-ro kom-prAr . . .

I would like . . .
  Quisiera . . .
  ki-syEh-ra

Do you have . . ?
  ¿Tiene . . ?
  tyEh-ne

buy TOCINO if you want breakfast
bacon. This is solid fat from the
pork belly, with no lean, and it is
for chopping and frying with
vegetables. Ask for *beicón*.
Butter quickly loses its pleasant
taste; margarine, sold in tubs,
makes a better spread.

Basic Stores

Bacon Beicón *beh-ee-kOn*
Biscuits Galletas *ga-lyEh-tas*
Bread, rolls Pan, panecillos *pAn,
pa-ne-thEE-lyos*
Cake Pastel *pAs-tel*
Cheese Queso *kEh-so*
Chocolate Chocolate *cho-ko-lA-te*
Coffee beans (ready ground) Café
en grano (molido) *ka-fEh en
grA-no (mo-IEE-do)*
Eggs Huevos *WEh-vos*
Flour Harina *a-rEE-na*
Ice-creams Helados *e-lA-dos*
Jam of any flavour (thick)
Mermelada *mer-me-lA-da*
Ketchup Salsa de tomate *SAl-sa
de to-mA-te*
Margarine Margarina, Tulipán
mar-ga-rEE-na, too-li-pAn
Milk Leche *lEh-che*
Oil (olive) Aceite (de oliva)
a-thEh-ee-te (de o-lEE-va)
Salt, black pepper, paprika Sal,
pimienta, pimentón dulce *sAhl,
pi-myEn-ta, pi-myen-tOn dOOl-the*
Sausages for frying Chorizos para
cocinar *cho-rEEthos pA-ra
ko-thi-nAr*
Sugar Azúcar *a-thOO-kar*
Sweets Caramelos *ka-ra-mEh-los*
Tea Té *tEh*
Vinegar (sherry) Vinagre (de
jerez) *vi-nA-gre de HE-reth*
Yoghurt Yogur *yo-gOOr*
Washing-up liquid Detergente
para la vajilla *de-ter-HEn-te pA-ra
la va-hEEl-lya*
Washing powder Jabón en polvo
ha-bOn en pOl-vo

BUYING MEAT AND POULTRY

As well as the useful 'spit-roast
chicken' stalls found in large
villages at the weekend, Spain
has special shops, called
pollerías for selling chickens
and eggs. Most supermarkets
and butchers also sell fresh and
frozen chicken.
A meat shop, *una carnicería*,
looked rather medieval until
recently, with lumps of meat on
hooks. Supermarkets still cut
meat to order. Spaniards eat
quite a lot of mince, in meatballs and stuffed vegetables.
Try the less-familiar veal mince,
or a mixture with pork or ham.
By the way, meat from the
bullfight is not sold in ordinary
butchers (see CARNE DE LIDIA).

Types of Meat

Ternera is a cross between beef
and veal, and makes good
chops and steaks. However,
most families eat pork as their
main meat. Small village shops
often have a chilled cabinet with
chops and a boned loin of pork
for slicing. Lamb is a luxury, and
chops most of all. Stewing lamb
is sold with all the bones in, but
is good. In the south, kebab
meat is sold ready-cubed and
marinated.
Raw ham is used a lot in Spanish
recipes. The cheapest type of
SERRANO (off the bone) is in the
cabinet with the cold meat and
a bit will be cut to order for you.
Think of the red CHORIZO as a
sausage with ketchup already in
it. It is much more meaty than
British sausages. The ones with
red string are often very hot
(*picante*) while white string
means they are mild. The
whitish BUTIFARRA is made from

veal or pork, for grilling, while LONGANIZA and black puddings like MORCILLA are for cutting up and flavouring bean dishes. You will also find a 'deli' section in most large butchers, selling cooked and ready-to-eat cured meat. These are listed under **Picnics** on page 97.

Types of Meat and Chicken to Cook

Minced meat (often beef) Carne picada *kAr-ne pi-kA-da*
Stewing beef from ox (cow) Carne de buey (vaca) *kAr-ne de booEh-y, (vA-ka)*
Beef fillet Solomillo *so-lo-mEE-lyo*
Pork tenderloin (fillet) Solomillo de cerdo *so-lo-mEE-lyo de thEr-do*
Pork (lamb) chops Chuletas de cerdo (cordero) *choo-lEh-tas de thEr-do (kor-dEh-ro)*

The Spanish enjoy good fresh fish, both eating out and at home

BUYING FISH

The Spanish love fish and eat it about three times a week. Spain has some of the best fish in Europe; it is sold fresh everywhere and there is a considerable choice. In the Cádiz area there are also *freidurías*, take-away fried fish shops.

The phrases on pages 94–5 will give you an idea of how different fish are bought for cooking. However, Spain is very regional: fish are called different names in different places, while one name can be used for several different fish. Fish are sorted by size – confusing, until you realise the same fish appears in different piles. Tiny sardines under 2cm (¾in) long are for deep frying, and the normal-size ones for grilling. Larger hake (*merluza*) are for cooking, but little ones (*pescadillas*) are for chopping up to make fish soup. Unsorted (mixed) prawns can be cheaper than sorted ones.

Basically, oily fish like mackerel are best grilled. If they look like meat steaks, such as swordfish or tuna, they needs lots of oil while grilling. Pinkish fleshed fish, sold skinned, need an acid marinade, or lemon juice and capers to serve. White fish can be cooked every way.

Grilling is easiest, while barbecuing is more fun, if you have outside space for a fire. Frying is easy for two, but hard work for more people, because there are rarely enough pans, or space, in a Spanish kitchen. Many Spanish recipes start fish in the pan and finish in the oven with a sauce. A thick fish soup is also a good bet.

Shellfish are sold raw and prawns need boiling – 3 minutes for *gambas* and 5–6 for *langostinos* and *cigalas*, depending on size. They are good eaten with coarse salt. Big

ones can be barbecued. Bigger clams are usually eaten raw, little ones included in soups and sauces.

Small freezer shops are common in villages and these stock open boxes of fish and of different vegetables. Here you can buy quantities as small as 100g (¼lb) to go in something like a *paella*. They also offer items like battered crab claws, fish in crumbs and little salted cod pies (*tortas de bacalao*). Don't buy BACALAO (salted cod) unless you can wait a day for it to soak. After that, it can be used like fresh fish. Salted sardines are sold packed in a fan shape in wooden boxes: rinse and use them. Many classic dishes, such as *bacalao a la purrusalda* (leek and salted cod soup) are also sold canned.

Fish for Cooking

Buying fish

I want fish for soup. Quiero pescados para sopa. *kyEh-ro pes-kA-dos pa-ra sO-pa*
For baking Para cocinar al horno *pa-ra ko-thi-nAr al Or-no*
Please clean them. Limpieles, por favor. *lEEm-pyeh-les por fa-vOr*
Without heads and filleted Sin cabezas, y en filetes *sin ka-bEh-thas, ee en fi-lEh-tes*

Whole fish for grilling

Bream with pink fins Besugo *be-sOO-go*
Bright pink red mullet Salmonetes *sal-mo-nEh-tes*
Sardines, (look 'sequined' if fresh) Sardinas *sar-dEE-nas*

Fish steaks for grilling, oiling frequently

Swordfish with black skin Pez espada *peth es-pA-da*

Crisp fried fish from Málaga

Tuna, very meaty flesh Atún
a-tOOn
White-fleshed tuna Bonito
bo-nEE-to

Fillets or fish steaks for cooking in wine
Hake Merluza *mer-lOO-tha*
Grouper Mero MEh-ro
Bream with yellow eyebrow
Dorado (expensive) *do-rA-do*
Monkfish, tail with 1 bone Rape
rAh-pe

Fish for frying
Sole, small and big Lenguado
len-gwA-do

BUYING CHEESE
The national cheeses are mainly hard and cheddar-like – and something of an acquired taste. MANCHEGO is the famous name and there are many other cheeses like it. An old, ripened cheese (*añejo*) will be very strong, crumbly and hard, a bit like Parmesan. The same cheese is softer and blander when young (*queso tierno*). You may be asked ¿*Queso de vaca o queso de cabra?*, Cows' milk cheese or goats'? as the country is famous for its sheep and goat cheeses. These are mainly hard or semi-hard cheeses too, all cut in slices from a drum-shape, and the main difference is that cows' milk cheese is a bit cheaper. Bland international cheeses like Edam are also widely sold. Firm Spanish cheeses grate well and the most successful cooked dish is *queso frito* – slices egged and crumbed, then fried. They are popular to start or end the meal. Many areas do make soft fresh cheeses, but they are not so easy to find; nor is cottage cheese, REQUESÓN. Soft CUAJADA (junket) is more widely distributed. Several cheeses are described in the **A-Z Guide to Spanish Foods**.

BUYING VEGETABLES AND FRUIT
You will find a good choice of vegetables in markets and in *una verdulería*, a greengrocer. The quality is exceptionally good, sizes are huge, colours bright and prices low.
Learn to use the vegetables available. Chard, with leaves like spinach, is worth a try, and whole artichokes, too. Look up how to eat them in the **A–Z Guide to Spanish Foods** if they are not familiar and then try them out. In summer, Spaniards love salads.

Vegetables
Artichoke (globe) Alcachofa
al-ka-chO-fa
Asparagus Espárragos
es-pAr-ra-gos
Aubergine Berenjena
be-ren-HEh-na
Broad beans Habas *A-bas*
Dried beans Alubias, judías
a-lOO-byas, Hoo-dEE-as
Cabbage, green Berza, repollo
bEr-tha, re-pO-lyo
Cabbage, red Lombardo
lom-bAr-do
Carrot Zanahoria *tha-na-O-rya*
Cauliflower Coliflor *ko-li-flOr*
Chard Acelga *a-thEl-ga*
Chick-peas Garbanzos
gar-bAn-thos
Courgette Calabacín
ka-la-ba-thEEn
Cucumber Pepino *pe-pEE-no*
Fennel Hinojo *ee-no-Ho*
Garlic Ajo *a-Ho*

Who can resist ripe strawberries?

Green beans Judías verdes *Hoo-dEE-as vEr-des*
Leek Puerro *pwEr-ro*
Lettuce Lechuga *le-chOO-ga*
Lentils Lentejas *len-tEh-Has*
Mushrooms (button) Champiñones *cham-pi-nyO-nes*
Mushrooms (wild) Setas *sEh-tas*
Olives Aceitunas *a-thEh-ee-tOO-nas*
Onion Cebolla *the-bO-lya*
Parsley Perejil *pe-re-HEEl*
Peas Guisantes *gwee-sAn-tes*
Pepper, green (red) Pimiento verde (rojo) *pi-myEn-to vEr-de, (rO-Ho)*
Potato Patata *pa-tA-ta*
Radishes Rábanos *rA-ban-os*
Spinach Espinacha *es-pi-nA-cha*
Spring onions Cebolletas *the-bo-lyEh-tas*
Sweet potato (orange yam) Batata (boniato) *ba-tA-ta (bo-nyA-to)*
Tomato Tomate *to-mA-te*
Watercress Berros *bEr-ros*

Fruit
Apple Manzana *man-thA-na*
Apricots Albaricoques *al-ba-ri-kO-kes*
Banana Plátano *plA-ta-no*
Cherries Cerezas *the-rEh-thas*
Dates Dátiles *dA-ti-les*
Figs (early) Higos (brevas) *EE-gos (brEh-vas)*
Grapefruit Pomelo *po-mEh-lo*
Grapes black (white) Uvas negras (blancas) *OO-vas nEh-gras (blAn-kas)*
Lemon Limón *li-mOn*
Orange Naranja *na-rAn-Ha*
Pear Pera *pEh-ra*
Pineapple Piña *pEE-nya*
Plums Ciruelas *thi-rwEh-las*
Pomegranate Granada *gra-nA-da*
Prunes Ciruelas pasas *thi-rwEh-las pA-sas*
Raspberries Frambuesas *fram-bwEh-sas*
Strawberries Fresas *frEh-sas*
Tangerine Mandarina *man-da-rEE-na*

Making Your Choice
Some (a little) . . . Un poco de . . . *oon pO-ko de*
A couple of jars (cans) Dos tarros (latas) *dos tAr-ros (lA-tas)*
A packet of . . . Un paquete de . . . *oon pa-kEh-te de*
In oil (brine) En aceite (salmuera) *en a-thEh-i-te (sahl-moo-Eh-ra)*
In one piece En un trozo *en oon trO-tho*
A slice (slab) of meat Un pedazo de carne *oon pe-dA-tho de kAr-ne*
Bigger, smaller Más grande, más pequeño *mas grAn-de, mas pe-kEh-nyo*
Can I help myself? ¿Puedo servirme? *pwEh-do ser-vEEr-me*
Don't touch! !No tocar! *no to-kAr*
Anything else? ¿Algo más? *al-go mAs*

That's it (no more) Nada más
NA-da mAs

Money and How to Pay
What does it cost? ¿Cuánto es?
kwAn-to es
This is the cheapest. Es el (la) más
barato(a) *es el (la) mAs ba-rA-to
(a)*
Go to the checkout (till). Pase por
caja *pA-se por kA-Ha*

PICNICS
The salads in Spain are so
delicious and varied that
shopping for picnics is a
positive pleasure.
The *bocadilla* is one of the
nicest sandwiches in the world.
Made from a crusty roll, it is
split and dribbled with olive oil,
instead of butter, which goes off
quickly in hot weather. Inside,
ham (SERRANO) and cheese are a
wonderful combination. PA AMB
TOMÀQUET, Catalan bread with
tomato juice pressed in, is also
very good.
There are many other picnic
ingredients to choose from.
Little cans full of seafood, sold
for starters, are particularly
good with salad, for example.
Vegetables in marinade, eaten
with a spoon from the can, are
excellent. Two of you can easily
finish a can.
Many cans have ring-pull
openers, but the big litre beer
bottles will need a bottle
opener!

Shopping for Picnics
Where are the drinks? ¿Dónde
están las bebidas? *dOn-de es-tAn
las be-bEE-das*
Do you have cold beers? ¿Tiene
cervezas frías? *tyEh-ne
ther-vEh-thas frEE-as*

Mineral water (fizzy drinks) Agua
mineral (gaseoso) *A-gwa
mi-ne-rAl (ga-se-O-so)*
Where can I buy a can-opener
(knife)? ¿Dónde se puede
comprar un abridor de latas
(cuchillo)? *dOn-de se pwEh-de
kom-prAr oon a-bri-dOr de lA-tas
(koo-chEE-lyo)*

COOKED MEAT
You will find cold meat in
supermarkets or in a
specialist *charcutería*. They
sell the familiar salamis and
mortadellas and Spanish cold
meats. The larger CHORIZOS,
about 5cm (?in) across, are for
slicing and eating raw. Many
pressed meats are made, half
minced, half in small pieces.
Pudín de cerdo is rather like
corned beef made of pork.
Spaniards eat a lot of ham. The
most expensive is raw SERRANO.
But cooked ham is sold
everywhere, while cured 'ham'
pieces of shoulder are good and
much cheaper.

Cold Meats
Do you have cold meats? ¿Tiene
fiambres? *tyEh-ne fyAm-bres?*
I want to buy slices. Quisiera
comprar tajadas. *ki-syEh-ra
kom-prAr ta-HA-das*
Cooked pork loin Lomo cocido,
adobado *LO-mo ko-thEE-do,
a-do-bA-do*
Cooked ham Jamón de York
Ha-mOn de jork
Pressed tongue Fiambre de
lengua *fyAm-bre de lEn-gwa*
Cold cooked turkey breast Pavo
solo *pA-vo sO-lo*
Salami-type sausage Salchichón
sal-chi-chOn
Canned pâté Pâté en lata *Pah-tEh
en lA-ta*

RECIPES

The recipes below vary in difficulty. Those with one star (*) are simple to prepare, while those with two stars (**) are more complex and time consuming.

*Huevos a la flamenca***

Baked Eggs with Gypsy Trimmings

Serves 4

Slices of sausage, bits of ham and prawns can all go into this dish – all together, if you like – for it is a colourful mixture of whatever comes to hand, baked in tomato sauce.

4 tablespoons olive oil
1 large onion, peeled and chopped
2 garlic cloves, skinned and finely chopped
2 *chorizo* sausages, sliced
100g/4oz sliced raw *serrano* ham, diced
1 large green pepper, destalked, seeded and diced
400g/14oz can tomatoes and juice
salt, pepper and paprika
100g/4oz cooked green beans, cut into short lengths
4 or 8 eggs

Heat the oven to High for butane gas (180°C, 350°F, gas mark 4 at home) and put in a *cazuela* or four ovenproof baking dishes. Heat the oil in a frying pan and fry the onion slowly until soft, then add the garlic. Fry the sausage and ham in the pan until cooked. Distribute them between the dish(es) in the oven.

Add the diced pepper to the pan and fry for 3–4 minutes. Empty the tomatoes into the pan, breaking them up with a spoon. Season with salt, pepper and a little paprika and cook until the tomato reduces to a sauce. Add the beans and heat through. Spoon the vegetable sauce over the sausage and ham. Break in one or two eggs per person, then just swirl them lightly into the sauce with a fork. Bake in the oven for about 15 minutes until the eggs are just set. Eat with bread and a green salad.

Note. At home you can use smoked gammon cut from a knuckle, which is cheap, instead of *serrano*. Chicken livers go well in it too.

*Tortilla de camarones***

Spanish Shrimp Omelette

Serves 4

Spanish omelettes are not like French ones, but more like cakes – the shape of a sponge layer. They are often cut like cakes, too, into wedges that go into sandwiches, or are spiked with cocktail sticks as tapas. A variety of things can go in them, cooked potato and fried onion being popular. But shrimps and small prawns almost always end up in fritters or tortillas, as they are too small to peel for a fish dish. Remember, in Spain they are raw, so need brief cooking.

300–350g/10–12oz raw shrimps
  or prawns
4 tablespoons olive oil
2 tablespoons chopped onion
1 small garlic clove, skinned
  and finely chopped
salt, pepper and paprika
8 large eggs

Start by peeling the shrimps – or delegate the job! Meanwhile heat 2 tablespoons of the oil in a frying pan, about 23cm/9 inches across, and fry the onion slowly until soft, adding the garlic at the end. Turn up the heat and add the shrimps. Cook for 2 minutes, stirring occasionally, then sprinkle with salt, pepper and paprika. Turn them into a large bowl.

Wipe the pan with kitchen paper and heat the remaining oil. Break the eggs on to the shrimps and stir together. Pour the egg mixture into the pan, distributing the shrimps well. Cook for 1 minute over high heat to set the bottom, then turn down to low. Use a spatula to pull the egg away from the side of the pan and make a straight side. To make sure the bottom is not sticking, shake the pan by pushing it away then pulling it back vigorously.

When the top starts to set, cover it with a plate and flip the pan over, to turn out the *tortilla*. Slide it back the other way up, and give it 2–3 more minutes to set. Tortilla should be quite chunky and solid. You can eat it with tomato sauce if you like.

Ingredients for shrimp tortilla

*Entremeses especialidades**

Three special starter salads

Salads are the backbone of summer lunches. Nice though tomato salad and lettuce are, it is a treat to have something special.

Pimientas con anchoas
Pimentos with Anchovy
Buy a couple of cans each of red pimentos and anchovies. Drain them both. Cut the pimentos into strips. Arrange on a plate and crisscross with anchovies. Good with cold

Potato and tuna salad

cooked beans in tomato sauce – which can also be bought canned.

Alcachofas y atún
Artichoke Hearts with Tuna
Tiny fluffy artichoke hearts (not the bases) are sold canned and frozen (the latter need brief cooking). Split them lengthways into three, and serve with canned tuna, mayonnaise and cold potatoes.

Pan y tomate con chorizo
Tomato-bread with Chorizo
The Catalans are so fond of this that I have included it, even though it seems too simple. Buy good crusty bread and cut into rounds. Cut ripe tomatoes in half, then crush on to the bread, so it becomes soaked with the juice. Dribble with a little olive oil; some people rub with a garlic clove, too. Top these with thin slices of CHORIZO which is sold for eating raw or SALCHICHÓN which has peppercorns in it.

*Ensaladilla de patatas y atún**

Potato Salad with Tuna and Capers

Serves 4

The secret of really good potato salad is to make it then eat it straight away. When the potatoes are still slightly warm, they seem to taste better. Any potato left over makes an extra item in a mixed salad. The Spanish invented anchovy-stuffed hard-boiled eggs, and these go well with it.

1kg/2lb new potatoes
¼ mild Spanish onion
2 (100g/4oz) cans tuna in oil
salt and pepper
300ml/½ pint mayonnaise
2 tablespoons drained capers

If the potatoes are small, boil them in their skins until cooked – usually about 20 minutes. If they are large, peel and cut into equal size chunks and cook, then drain well in a colander. Peel as soon as they are cool enough to handle and chop into a shallow salad bowl.

Chop the onion and scatter over the potatoes. Empty the tuna and its oil into the potatoes and break up the fish with a fork. Sprinkle with salt and pepper and turn gently. Add enough mayonnaise to coat the potatoes to your taste, then sprinkle with capers and serve.

*Garbanzos en salsa de tomate***

Chick-peas in Tomato Sauce

Serves 4

Chick-peas look a little like hazelnuts when they have been soaked, and have a bit of a nutty taste too. They are the potatoes of Spain, eaten hot to fill you up – and cold and salted as a snack with beer, like potato crisps. This basic recipe goes well with fried or grilled sausages, while you try out the local chorizos and butifarras, to discover which ones you prefer. A little chopped serrano, or pancetta which is like streaky bacon, is good fried in it with the onion. You can eat this stew cold with salad, or put it into a tortilla (see recipe on page 98). Or eat chick-peas a favourite Spanish way, with hot cooked spinach stirred in.

500g/1lb dried chick-peas (or 1kg/2lb ready-soaked)
2 tablespoons olive oil
1 mild Spanish onion, peeled and chopped
1 green pepper, destalked, seeded and chopped
2 garlic cloves, skinned and finely chopped
800g/1lb 12oz can whole or chopped tomatoes
1 tablespoon paprika
2 tablespoons wine vinegar
pepper and salt

Soak the chick-peas overnight, if necessary (see note). Heat the oil in a flameproof casserole and gently fry the onion until soft, adding the green pepper and garlic towards the end. Add the tomatoes and their juice, chopping them a little with a spoon, if they are whole. Add the soaked chick-peas. Stir in the paprika and vinegar, and add pepper to taste.

Bring to the boil, cover and simmer, stirring occasionally. Spanish chick-peas cook in about an hour (at home Greek chick-peas need 2 hours), but longer won't hurt them, and they reheat well. Check occasionally to see that they are still covered with liquid and stir. Add salt to taste before serving. This stew is particularly good with *chorizo picantes*.

Note. In Spain, chick-peas are sold ready-soaked on delicatessen counters. But there are two ways to soak them yourself. Either cover the chick-peas well with three times the volume of cold water and leave overnight. Or pour boiling water over them and leave for one hour.

*Alcachofas salteadas con jamón***

Sautéed Artichoke Bases with Ham

Serves 4

Artichokes are always in the market, but many people don't know what to do with them, or find them fiddly to eat whole. This is an easy way to eat them fresh. You can also make this popular dish with canned (and in Spain frozen) bases, or cooked broad beans or fresh peas. At home a 500g/1lb bag of frozen broad beans is perfect. Buy the cheaper serrano *ham for cooking, not the best slices, which are carved from the bone for* tapas.

Artichokes with ham

8 globe artichokes
2 tablespoons olive oil
1 onion, peeled and finely
    chopped
2 garlic cloves, skinned and
    finely chopped
250g/8oz raw *serrano* ham *para
    cocinar*, cubed
salt and pepper
chopped fresh parsley
    (optional)

To prepare the artichokes, chop off the stalks (if they are stringy, that means the artichokes are tough and will need an extra 5 minutes' cooking). Trim the bottom so it is flat, removing small leaves. Turn on its side and cut through the top leaves, leaving a base about 4cm/1½ inches deep. Trim away the side leaves with a small knife until the white base shows through. Cook the bases in boiling salted water for 10 minutes. Drain upside down and cool briefly.

Flip off any soft leaf stumps with your thumb, revealing the choke. Use a spoon and your thumb to remove and discard the bristly choke, leaving a smooth saucer-shaped base. The bases need about 5 minutes' more cooking, either in a frying pan (as in this dish), or in boiling water if you want to use them for salad.

Heat the oil in a frying pan and cook the onion until softened, adding the garlic near the end. Add the ham, tossing over high heat for 1–2 minutes. Quarter the artichoke bases, add them to the pan and fry for about 5 minutes, stirring occasionally. Season and serve garnished with parsley, if you can buy it.

*Sopa de pescados y mariscos con naranjas***

Fish Soup with Orange

Serves 4

Many people don't like bones on their plates, so this is a good way to serve only the fillets, yet use the heads, bones and skins that you have paid for. It is also fun to eat and to shop for. Look at the fish as you are buying them and imagine that about one third (from the middle of the back) will be bone-free white flesh, and the rest can go to make the soup part. Get the fishmonger to do the chopping for you: 'limpieles, por favor.' *Shellfish that look interesting but fiddly to open, can go in and will be no problem. The stalks (not heads) of parsley can go in too, and also any of those recognisable herbs that get picked on holiday walks because they smell nice.*

2kg/4½lb mixed fish with heads
2 large Spanish onions, peeled and chopped
2 bay leaves
small bunch parsley
handful of herbs, even wild lavender
2 tablespoons olive oil
1 green pepper, destalked, seeded and chopped
2 large garlic cloves, skinned and fincly chopped
2 tablespoons flour
200ml/7fl oz dry white wine
salt, pepper and paprika
your choice of: 200g/7oz prawns and/or little clams, small crabs, etc
1 large tomato, skinned and seeded, flesh chopped
½ dried chilli (*quindilla*) or a little cayenne
8 small new potatoes (optional)
1 orange

Identify the best bits of the fish and chop these out quickly, if this hasn't been done. No need to be fussy about this, as all the rest is used. Keep the flesh aside on a plate. Put the heads, bones, skin, etc in a large saucepan or flameproof casserole with 1 chopped onion and the bay leaves. Cut off and scrumple up the parsley stalks and add them and any herbs. Cover with 1.2 litres/2 pints water and bring to the boil. Simmer for 40 minutes, then strain off the stock.

Heat the oil in a pan, large enough to take everything and

fry the remaining onion slowly until soft. Add the chopped pepper, then the garlic. Sprinkle with flour and cook for 1 minute, stirring, then add the wine. Season the reserved fish pieces with salt, pepper and paprika and tuck these into the pan, with any little crabs, prawns, clams, etc. Add the chopped tomato flesh and chilli and potatoes (if using). These should be small or cubed to the size of big marbles. Cut the zest from the orange in a spiral with a potato peeler and add. Squeeze the orange juice. Pour in 1 litre/1¾ pints fish stock and bring to simmering point. Cover and cook over low heat for 20 minutes, then add the orange juice. Check the seasoning and add parsley.
Note: For a party at home, the stock can be strained off and 2 tablespoons rice cooked in it. Serve this first, garnished with chopped prawns and parsley. Serve the fish with boiled new potatoes as a main course.

Fish soup with orange

Cigalas a la parrilla con alioli**

Grilled Scampi with Garlic 'Mayonnaise'

Serves 4

This is terribly messy to eat, so a good dish to serve when everyone is in bathing suits. The sauce is very strong, too – not for anyone who does not like garlic. But it is also the best accompaniment for grills, and Spaniards serve it with grilled lamb chops and even roast lamb.

1kg/2lb raw scampi without heads
a little olive oil
coarse salt
For the alioli
6 garlic cloves, skinned
½ teaspoon salt
2 egg yolks
200ml/7fl oz good olive oil

Make the *alioli* first. Chop the garlic really finely, then sprinkle with the salt. Use the flat side of a table knife to mash it to a paste – or use a pestle and mortar. Put the egg yolks in a bowl and stir in the garlic.

In a Spanish kitchen there is no danger of cold oil, but if you are at home, stand the jug of measured oil in a pan of warm water for a few minutes. Whisk the egg yolks, preferably with an electric whisk, and add a few drops of oil. When these have been incorporated, add a few more – the mayonnaise should thicken quickly. As soon as it thickens, you can start adding the oil faster, beating all the time, until it is incorporated. If you keep the sauce in the refrigerator, place in a screw-top jar or keep well covered.

Light the barbecue and let the fire die down, or heat the grill to high. Brush the scampi with oil and grill for about 8–10 minutes, depending on their size. Transfer them to a dish and scatter with coarse salt.

The neat way to get scampi out of their shells is to pick one up from the back and press the sides together. This cracks the shell all down the stomach. You can get a thumb under the legs on one side and peel them upwards, to take off a bit of the back shell – like taking off a saddle. After that, pinch the tail fin hard and pull the body. It should pop out when the vacuum is released. To eat, dunk the scampi in the sauce. Plenty of serviettes will be needed.

*Merluza a la vasca***

Hake in Wine and Seafood Sauce

Serves 4

Any white fish can be used for this dish, which is liked by children, because the fish doesn't have too many bones. It is finished in the oven, and you can use a big cazuela or one ovenproof dish per person, which is easier. It is good, too, with frozen peas substituted for the shellfish, but be sure then to include the parsley.

4 tablespoons olive oil
250g/8oz onions, peeled and chopped
2 big garlic cloves, skinned and finely chopped
4 tablespoons flour
salt and pepper
1 teaspoon paprika
4 hake steaks or fish fillets, 700g/1½ lb
1 medium tomato
300ml/½ pint dry white wine
200ml/7fl oz water with a fish cube, or fish stock
1 bay leaf
250g/8oz baby clams or prawns, peeled
chopped fresh parsley to garnish (optional)

Heat the oven to High for butane gas (180°C, 350°F, gas mark 4 at home). Heat the oil in a frying pan and fry the onions slowly until soft, then add the garlic. Put the flour on a plate and sprinkle with salt, pepper and paprika. Take any loose bones out of the fish, then coat the pieces in the seasoned flour.

RECIPES

Push the onion to the sides of the pan and put in the fish, frying it until golden – about 4 minutes each side. Transfer the fish pieces to an ovenproof dish or dishes and put them in the oven.

Peel the tomato while the fish is frying: ripe skin should strip off easily. Quarter it, then scoop out and discard the seeds. Chop the flesh and add to the pan with a little of the wine. Reduce this, stirring occasionally. Add the remaining wine and water (or stock) and crumbled stock cube if using, plus the bay leaf, and bring back to the boil. Pour over the fish. If individual dishes are being used, you may need a little more liquid. Tuck the clams or prawns round the fish pieces and return to the oven. Reduce the oven temperature (to 160°C, 325°F, gas mark 3 at home) and leave the dish for 10 minutes or so. Serve sprinkled with parsley and eat with crusty bread.

*Paella Valenciana***

Mixed Rice with Chicken and Seafood

Serves 4

Eat paella in a restaurant when you are in Spain: they have the pans and space. It is quite hard work to prepare yourself. However, you must have a recipe to take home, to remind you of your holiday. Best to take the rice home too. This is the easy version, but even so it takes over an hour.

4–5 tablespoons olive oil
1 onion, peeled and chopped
2 garlic cloves, skinned and finely chopped
700ml/1 pint 4fl oz good stock
200ml/7fl oz dry white wine
30 saffron strands or 2g sachet saffron powder
250g/8oz little squid (or mussels, cleaned)
250g/8oz raw prawns, peeled
salt, pepper and cayenne
4 chicken thighs, or 2 legs, split in half
400g/14oz Spanish medium-grain rice (or Italian risotto rice)
1 teaspoon paprika
100g/4oz cooked green beans or peas
200g/7oz canned red pimento, drained
chopped fresh parsley

Use two pans to speed frying – a *paella* pan or wide shallow flameproof casserole big enough to take the complete dish, plus a frying pan. Heat 2 tablespoons of the oil in the *paella* pan and fry the onion gently until soft, adding the garlic at the end.

Next, warm the stock and wine, then pour a little of this liquid over the saffron in a cup. Prepare the shellfish. To clean squid, first use the tentacles to pull out everything inside, then cut off the heads above the eyes. Discard everything except the tentacles and body. Flex the body to pop our the transparent 'spine'. Wash well, rubbing off the skin, and cut the body into rings.

Heat 2 more tablespoons oil in the second pan and put in the squid tentacles and rings. Fry

for a couple of minutes, then remove to a plate. Put in the peeled prawns and fry for 2 minutes, then transfer to the plate with the squid. Rub salt, pepper and cayenne into the chicken pieces. Add more oil to the pan if necessary, then add the chicken pieces and fry for about 10 minutes on each side. Meanwhile, wash the rice in a sieve and drain. When the onion is ready, add the rice to the *paella* pan and stir into the onion. Fry for a couple of minutes, stirring, then sprinkle with the paprika. Add the saffron liquid and one-third of the stock and bring to the boil. Start timing now – for 20 minutes. When the liquid has been absorbed, add another third of the stock and evenly distribute the chicken, squid, prawns and beans or peas round the paella pan. When the liquid has nearly gone, add the remaining liquid and give the mixture a stir. Move the chicken pieces, bedding them into the liquid round the pan. The liquid should all disappear, and cooking time should be up about 6–7 minutes later. Test that the rice is cooked. Cut the pimento into strips and lay these across the rice. Turn off the heat and wrap the *paella* pan in foil then newspaper, to keep in the steam. Let it stand for 10 minutes. The flavours will blend and the last drop of liquid should disappear. Sprinkle with parsley and serve. Spaniards prefer red wine with *paella*.
Note. Packs of small, frozen squid are often sold in larger supermarkets in the UK.

The classic dish of Spain: paella

Gambas pil-pil*

Sizzling Hot Prawns

Serves 4

Everybody loves these, but you must adjust the amount of chilli according to your preference. A whole fresh chilli, dried chillies or a tiny amount of cayenne or paprika can be used.

8–12 tablespoons olive oil
350g/12oz raw prawns in the
   shell
1 fresh chilli, or 2 dried chillies,
   or ¼ teaspoon cayenne, or
   1 teaspoon paprika
2 garlic cloves, skinned and
   chopped
salt

Heat the oven to High for butane gas (220°C, 425°F, gas mark 7 at home). Pour 2–3 tablespoons oil each – Spaniards like more – into four individual ovenproof dishes (*cazuelitas*) and heat them in the oven. Meanwhile, peel the prawns. If you are using fresh chilli, remove the stalk and seeds, then slice into fine rings. Deseed dried chillies and crush into tiny pieces. Distribute the garlic in the oil and add the fresh or dried chilli. Divide the prawns between the dishes and sprinkle with salt (and cayenne or paprika if using), then stir in the oil. Return to the oven for 5 minutes until really hot. Serve with cocktail sticks for picking up the prawns and plenty of good bread for mopping up the juices.

Gambas pil-pil: *hot prawns flavoured with garlic and chilli*

*Pollo al chilindrón***

Fried Chicken with Ham and Red Peppers

Serves 4

This is Spain's most popular fried chicken dish, named after a card game. It might seem extra trouble grilling the peppers, but it fits in nicely with the frying time. Cooked like this they are a basic Spanish ingredient, sweet and juicy, and make a lovely puréed sauce.

2 red peppers
2 tablespoons olive oil
1 onion, peeled and finely chopped
salt, pepper and paprika
4 chicken quarters
100g/4oz raw *serrano* ham, cubed
2 garlic cloves, skinned and finely chopped
1 tomato, skinned and seeded

Heat the grill to high with the peppers on the rack. Grill them for 20 minutes, turning the peppers a quarter of the way over every 5 minutes. The skins will blacken. Place the hot peppers in a plastic bag and leave until they are cool enough to handle – 10 minutes – when the skins will come off easily. Peel off the skins on a plate, saving the juices. Split the peppers open and scoop out the seeds, discard these and the stalks.

Meanwhile heat the oil in a flameproof casserole and fry the onion slowly until soft. Rub salt, pepper and paprika into the chicken. Push the onion to the side of the pan and add the chicken pieces, frying them about 15 minutes on each side, until rosy and golden. About 5 minutes before they are ready, add the ham and garlic.

Chop the peppers on a plate, then mash with a fork. Chop the tomato flesh with it and add both to the spaces in the pan. Stir, cover, turn down the heat and cook for 10 minutes. Check the seasoning of the sauce and serve. New potatoes go well.

Pollo al ajillo a la parrilla*

Barbecued or Grilled Garlic Chicken

Serves 4

Spanish chickens taste as they are meant to, and this is an easy, but classic, way to eat them. Fish like besugo (one for two), *pretty pink salmonetes (one each), or about four sardinas per person can be cooked in the same way, adjusting times.*

1 chicken, cut into 4 serving pieces and backbone removed, or 8 thigh portions, or 4 legs
6 garlic cloves, skinned and finely chopped
2 teaspoons salt
1 teaspoon dried thyme (optional)
4 tablespoons olive oil
2 tablespoons lemon juice
thin strip of lemon zest, finely chopped
freshly ground black pepper

It is easier to cook chicken breasts if the two end wing joints are removed, leaving only one. Remove excess skin and prick the thick parts of the flesh with a fork, then put the chicken in a shallow dish. Chop the garlic and then heap it up and cover with the salt. With flat side of a table knife, crush the garlic into the salt until you have a paste. Put it in a cup and add the thyme, oil, and lemon juice and lemon zest. Spoon this over the chicken, peppering it and turning the pieces several times. Leave aside.

Light the barbecue, then let the flames die down to cook. Or heat the grill to high. Cook the chicken, turning it several times, for about 15 minutes on each side, dribbling or brushing with the marinade.

Note. A warning! Do not put the cooked chicken back into the unwashed marinade dish, to serve. There is always the risk of transferring salmonella from uncooked to cooked meat.

RECIPES

Solomillo de cerdo con maccarones**

Roast Pork with Sherry and Macaroni

Serves 4

This dish from the Cádiz region is so easy to cook and to shop for. A tenderloin of pork is economical, while a four-chop loin, boned and with rind removed, is more generous with the meat.

400g/14oz pork tenderloin or
    600g/1¼lb boned loin
3 garlic cloves, squashed
½ teaspoon salt
1 teaspoon paprika
pepper
4 tablespoons oil
250g/8oz macaroni
125ml/4fl oz *amontillado* sherry

Heat the oven to High for butane gas (190°C, 375°F, gas mark 5 at home). Rub the meat with the garlic cloves and then with salt, paprika and pepper. Put the garlic cloves into an oven dish, into which the pork fits snugly. Pour in the oil, then turn the pork in this. Roast a tenderloin for 35 minutes and a loin for 1 hour 10 minutes, basting after 15 minutes.
Meanwhile, bring a large pan of salted water to the boil. Add the macaroni and cook for 8–10 minutes, following packet instructions. At the same time, pour the sherry over the meat and baste again. When the meat is done, remove from the dish and discard the garlic. Drain the macaroni and add it to the

meat dish. Season well and stir so the macaroni is well coated with meat juices. Carve the pork into slices and lay it on top.
Note. At home buy a four-chop joint, about 800g/1¾lb, and have it skinned, boned, rolled and tied.

Chuletas de cerdo con alcaparras y pimiento*

Pork Chops with Capers and Peppers

Serves 4

More capers are produced in Spain than any other country. When pickled they have just the acidity to balance fried food, as in this colourful pepper and caper mixture. Try it, too, with fried fish.

2 tablespoons olive oil
1 small onion, peeled and
    chopped
1 green pepper, destalked,
    seeded and chopped
1 red pepper, destalked,
    seeded and chopped
1 garlic clove, skinned and
    finely chopped
4 pork chops
1 teaspoon paprika
salt and pepper
2 tablespoons pickled capers

Heat the oil in a frying pan large enough to take the chops and fry the onion gently for 10 minutes. Add the chopped peppers and garlic and fry, stirring occasionally, until the onions are soft – about another

10 minutes. Sprinkle the chops with paprika – standard practice in Spain – and the salt and pepper. Fry in the pan, pushing the vegetable mixture to the sides, or piling it on top of the chops, until these are well-cooked on both sides. Roughly chop the capers, stir into the peppers and heat through. Good with fried paprika potatoes. A Rioja *reserva* would complement the dish. Or try a Valdepeñas red; the better ones are made with Cenibel – the best Rioja grape.

*Cerdo con guisantes y champiñones en jerez***

Pork with Peas and Mushrooms in Sherry Sauce

Serves 4

An easy dish for spring or early summer. Boned pork loin is widely available and makes two neat slices each. Veal is good too, but more expensive; ask for filetitos, which are tiny escalopes. Fino in Spain also comes from Montilla, and so is not sherry, but is well liked for cooking.

3–4 tablespoons olive oil
2 tablespoons chopped onion
salt and pepper
600g/1¼lb boneless pork loin, sliced into 8 escalopes
2 garlic cloves, skinned and chopped
250g/8oz button mushrooms, cleaned and sliced
2 tablespoons flour
175ml/6fl oz *fino* or dry sherry
1.5kg/3lb peas in the pod, shelled
about 175ml/6fl oz stock, made with a cube

Heat 3 tablespoons oil in a flameproof casserole and put in the onion. Cook slowly until soft, then push the onion to the sides of the pan. Salt and pepper the

Pork with peas and sherry

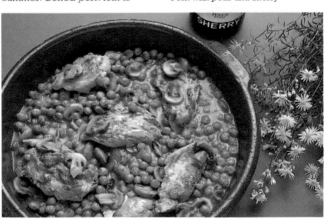

RECIPES

pork slices and fry these, over a high heat, until browned on both sides. Remove to a plate.
Add more oil, if needed, and the garlic and mushrooms. Cook more slowly, stirring occasionally until they soften. Sprinkle with the flour and stir this in. Add the *fino* and bring gently to the boil. Return the meat to the pan, distributing it well, then add the peas. Pour in just enough stock to cover. Bring to the boil and simmer for 20 minutes, covered, until both meat and peas are done.
Note. This is really a dish to show off fresh peas. However, frozen peas can be used; cook for 10 minutes only. Use brown (chestnut) mushrooms if you can get them.

*Sorbete de limón***

Lemon Sorbet

Serves 4

When it is so hot that all you want to do is sit in the shade and eat ice-cream, this is the freshest and most delicious ice of all. In restaurants, it is served spooned back into the lemon shells.

3–4 lemons
200g/7oz sugar
500ml/18fl oz water
2 large egg whites

Take strips of zest from the lemons with a potato peeler and put them in a saucepan with the sugar and water. Bring to the boil, then boil for 5 minutes without stirring. Cool and strain. Squeeze the lemon juice and add.
Turn the lemon liquid into a freezerproof container and freeze for about 2 hours until slushy. Beat with a fork, then freeze again for about 30 minutes. Remove from the freezer and beat again. Whisk the egg whites until soft peaks form and fold into the ice. Freeze again for about 1 hour.
Note: At home – or if you are lucky enough to have an electric mixer on holiday – leave the ice until almost stiff. Then put it in the mixer and whisk it. Add the whisked egg whites in large dollops. This is whisked into the ice, which will go almost white. You can eat the sorbet immediately or refreeze it.

Lemon sorbet, light and cooling

Sangría*

Chilled Red Wine and Citrus Fruit Punch

Serves 4

Some sangrías *contain brandy, but I think the nicest ones, on a hot day, are those that are quite light. In the south, where this drink is most often made, the red wines are very high in alcohol – lethal when it's sunny! This* sangría *is quite sweet, the way the Spanish like it. If you use soda water instead of fizzy lemon, stir in a couple of tablespoons of caster sugar first.*

8–10 ice cubes
4 oranges
2 lemons
½ cinnamon stick or 1 teaspoon
   ground cinnamon
1 litre bottle red wine, well
   chilled
750ml/1¼ pints fizzy lemonade,
   well chilled

Put the ice cubes into a jug that will hold at least 2 litres/3½

Sangría, *red wine punch*

pints. Take a thin strip of zest from one orange and one lemon. Add these, with the cinnamon, to the jug. Squeeze and add all the juice, with the red wine. Chill in the refrigerator for a couple of hours. Top up with fizzy lemonade just before serving.

Limonada fresca*

Lemonade

Even quite small children can make this themselves. It is full of vitamin C and a fraction of the price of bought drinks. One particular brand of flower honey in Spain is sold with a snap-shut pourer, which is ideal for this. For 1 glass, squeeze the juice from 1 lemon and pour into a tall glass with 2–3 ice cubes. Add 1 tablespoon sugar or honey, then top up with cold water. Stir and drink.

SPECIAL EVENTS

Spanish festivals are enormous fun, since they are mainly celebrated on the street. But they disrupt shopping and banks, and restaurants may be closed just before them, and are booked up during them.

The Spanish Tourist Office publishes a brochure every year, called the *Calendar of Celebrations*, with the dates of the main ones. However, almost every village celebrates its own saint's day.

The two public holidays that catch tourists unawares are Corpus Christi, the second Thursday after Whit Sunday and Assumption, which is 15 August. If the latter falls on a Thursday, shops may be shut for four days. Since Saturday is a working day in Spain for many, a Tuesday or Friday holiday is usually added to the weekend. Also many shops shut in August for a month's holiday.

Little cakes are the universal festival foods, but sadly few are of any distinction. However, you will find exceptional roasts on festival menus, suckling pig and in particular baby lamb and kid at Easter, and pies called PANADES in Mallorca.

Fruit and vegetables are seasonal. In spring you cannot buy red peppers, for example, and there may be a glut of green beans or peas, which then vanish.

San José on 19 March is celebrated in Valencia with the Fallas processions, and in Madrid with BUÑUELOS, while Lent and particularly Good Friday brings out a host of BACALAO dishes. San Jorge (St George's day) falls on 23 April, and many places in Valencia and Alicante, and Alcoy in particular, celebrate Spanish victory over the Moors with a simple rice and bean dish, MOROS Y CRISTIANOS.

April food specialities are wild asparagus (ESPÁRRAGOS TRIGUEROS) in the south and fresh palm hearts, cut from small palmettos. Loquats (NISPEROS) are in season and Easter sees the opening of the strawberry season.

Madrid celebrates its patron, San Isidore, around 15 May with BUÑUELOS and a fortnight-long festival. Corpus Christi, on the second Thursday after Whitsun, is marked by processions in Toledo, the MAZAPÁN city, and in Sitges, near Barcelona.

San Juan on 22 June is celebrated with bonfires and feasting, particularly in Alicante, while Pamplona-Irunea toasts San Fermin on 6–14 July with bullrunning.

Spain's National Day is 25 July, the Santiago Apóstal (St James), celebrated particularly in Valencia and, of course, in Santiago de Compostela, where TARTA DE SANTIAGO is eaten.

Asunción on 15 August means village festivals all over the south, with processions, flamenco and TURRÓN stalls.

The biggest festival for San Matteo and America Day on 19 September is in Oviedo. This date is also the focus for the grape harvest festivals, which happen before picking in all the major wine-making places like Jerez de la Frontera, Logroño in Rioja and Requena in Valencia. In Logroño, trestle tables are set up in the streets. Here baby lamb chops are grilled over vine prunings (*sarmiento*) and served with *lots* of wine! September is also the start of the wild mushroom season. SETAS are a national passion and appear on all the menus. An unusual cultivated vegetable, CARDO (cardoon) is eaten until Christmas.

The 12 October Pilar festival in Zaragoza is one of Spain's biggest, celebrating the Virgin. It is also Columbus Day. Round the same time, in mid-October, saffron is harvested in New Castile, with a celebration choosing a saffron queen.

On 1 November, *Todos Los Santos*, the only shops open are pastry shops selling HUESOS DE SANTO, or PANELLETS in Catalunya. The weeks before Christmas see TURRÓN, *figuritas de* MAZAPÁN and ROSCON DE REYES (yeast cake) on sale.

EATING OUT

The Spanish Day

Though Spaniards eat a light breakfast, you may want to stoke up with fruit and eggs, because lunch is normally eaten late. If you are going out to lunch, remember that Spaniards expect to eat between 14.00 and 16.00 hours – and this is the main meal of the Spanish day. Supper is then of the soup and eggs sort.

Where to Go?

There is no shortage of cafés and bars in Spain. In simple *tascas* it is standing only, but elsewhere you can sit. All have a choice of hot food.

Both smart *restaurantes* and the more modest *hosterías* (inns)

Taking a break

may well offer local dishes (*platos típicos*) and there is surprisingly little difference between the types of dishes in the two places. The state-run tourist hotels, the *paradores*, have a policy of offering local food, often in historic buildings. At festivals and in mid-season these become booked, but normally they have room.

A *marisquería* specialises in shellfish, while a *merendero* is a casual outdoor eatery, often serving fish. Popular beaches also have *tascas* serving drinks and some food. The modest roadside *venta* (which means 'sale') usually sells hot food as well as drinks and ices.

For afternoon tea, many *pastelerías* (pastry shops) also have a few tables; while you might find a *salón de té*. Cafés specialise in coffee, beer and ice-creams rather than food.

Beach bars provide basic snacks for hard-pressed sunbathers

Eating Through the Day

A bar is the place to buy breakfast in Spain, usually a quick affair of coffee and bread, though some specialise in chocolate and CHURROS. Early risers may then have a snack mid-morning, for lunch is late, rarely before 14.00 hours and often as late as 16.00 hours. Children have a *merienda*, (snack) when they come home from school, and adults may have a beer or pastry. *Tapas* (bar snacks) start about 19.00 hours, to fill in time before dinner or supper. This will be a lighter meal, eaten around 21.00 hours at home or in the country in the north. The south keeps later hours, 22.00 or 23.00 hours in town, and later still in Madrid.

Meals Through the Day

We would like something to eat.
Quisieramos algo para comer.
Ki-sye-rA-mos Al-go pa-ra ko-mEr
Lunch El almuerzo *el al-mwEr-tho*
Meal, usually lunch La comida *la ko-mEE-da*
Aperitifs (and snacks in general) Aperitivos *a-pe-ri-tEE-vos*
Bar snacks Tapas *tA-pas*

Dinner, supper La cena *la thEh-na*
Buffet or 'open table' La mesa franca, buffet *la mEh-sa frAn-ka, boo-fEt*

Eating Tapas

Tapas (bar snacks) are served with all drinks. They used to be free, and marinated olives and salted nuts may still be 'on the house', but you will have to pay for other snacks.

Cheese, raw ham and CHORIZO on bread are basic, as is cold potato ENSALADILLA and fried squid (CALAMARES) in the south. Prawns are universal (and expensive) and on the north coast there will be potted crab and clams and mussels in wine. Fried fish is popular in the south – try shark in batter (CAZÓN) for a change! All sorts of good things are deep fried – croquettes and cheesy puffs with vegetables or ham. Then there are varieties of things in sauce, like meatballs and tripe (CALLOS): portions are heated in the microwave. Finally there is chicken in garlic and miniature pork kebabs – PINCHOS – whose name is used to mean a *tapa*. In popular bars a large selection is laid out under glass for inspection. *Vamos de pinchos* means 'We're going out looking for *tapas*' – a *tapas* crawl! For just a tiny sample, ask for *una tapa. Una ración* is a more substantial portion, enough for two or three to share – or a cheap way of eating out quickly.

Making a Reservation

What time do you serve meals? ¿A qué hora se come? *a kEh O-ra se kO-me*

I want to reserve a table for four (six) people. Quiero reservar una mesa para cuatro (seis) personas. *kyEh-ro re-ser-vAr oo-na MEh-sa para kwA-tro (sEh-is) per-sO-nas*

I prefer non-smoking. Prefiero no fumadores. *pre-fyEh-ro no foo-ma-dO-res*

Is there a car park? ¿Hay aparcamiento? *A-ee a-par-ka-myEn-to*

The Spanish Lunch

Restaurant meals are usually leisurely. If you are in any sort of hurry, the set menu will come faster. Cooking methods in Spain tend to be straightforward, portions are enormous and almost everything is served with bread to mop up the juices. There is very little highly spiced food – though your plate may end up covered with bones from either meat or fish.

Soup or salads, then egg dishes or vegetables, are served as separate courses before the main course.

A popular soup is made of shellfish (*sopa de mariscos*). Soup may be based on clear broth from the stockpot (*caldo*) or may be a *potaje*, thick with vegetables. *Sopa de cebollas, espárragos* or *champiñones* (onion, asparagus or mushroom soup) is just as likely to be canned as it is at home. *Entremés de carne* is a selection of cold meats, but *ensalada mixta*, salad with tomato and tuna, is one of the most popular starters. Salads are put on the table before the main course, rather than after it, or as side dishes.

Egg dishes such as TORTILLA, which is not an omelette but more like a cake of egg, and HUEVOS A LA FLAMENCA, eggs in a wonderful mixed vegetable sauce (see recipes pages 98–99), make a main dish if you are not hungry. PAELLA and pasta dishes are also considered starters. Vegetable dishes tend to be massive, while the bean dishes are soupy stews, with plenty of liquid and a meal in themselves.

Fish cooked *a la plancha* is from the griddle, *a la parrilla* it is grilled (often on charcoal), while *la barbacoa* means an outside grill. If you prefer fish with sauce, try MERLUZA EN SALSA VERDE, or A LA VASCA (see recipe page 105). Meat, poultry and fish used to be served by themselves, with bread, though now many dishes come with potato chips. Fried and roast chicken (*pollo frito* or *asado*) and pork chops (*chuletas de cerdo*) are universal. But lamb chops (*chuletas de cordero*) are more of a luxury. If the restaurant advertises its oven outside, *un horno* (an old-fashioned bread oven), the roast lamb will be a real treat. *Una caldereta* is a stew.

Spaniards mainly close a meal with fruit; in general the desserts, pastries and ice-creams are not good. However, the classics like CREMA CATALANA and TOCINO DE CIELO can be delicious and are worth trying once. The cheese selections are not large, while soft cheeses may be served with honey or sugar as a dessert. A finishing sweet touch to a meal is more likely to come from a COÑAC (brandy) which is usually sweet and often perfumed.

EATING OUT

Understanding the Menu

The menu, please La carta (lista), por favor. *la kAr-ta (lEEs-ta) por fa-vOr*

Dish of the day Plato del día *plA-to del dEE-a*

Soups Sopas *sO-pas*

First course Primero plato *pri-mEh-ro plA-to*

Starters Entremeses *en-tre-mEh-ses*

Salads Ensaladas *en-sa-lA-das*

Egg dishes Huevos *wEh-vos*

Vegetables Legumbres, verduras *le-gOOm-bres, ver-dOO-ras*

Pasta dishes Pastas *pAs-tas*

Rice dishes Arroz, arroces *ar-rOth, ar-rO-thes*

Seafood Mariscos *ma-rEEs-kos*

Fish Pescados *pes-kA-dos*

Grills Parrilladas *par-ril-lya-das*

From the barbecue De barbacoa *de bar-ba-kO-a*

Meat Carnes *kAr-nes*

Cold dishes Platos fríos *plA-tos frEE-os*

Cheeses Quesos *kEh-sos*

How is it Cooked?

How is it cooked? ¿Cómo se hace? *kO-mo se A-the*

Baked Al horno *al Or-no*

Roast Asado *a-sA-do*

Fried Frito *frEE-to*

Battered and deep-fried A la romana *a la ro-mA-na*

Cooked on the grill A la parrilla *a la parEEl-lya*

Sautéed Salteado *sal-teh-A-do*

Marinated and (usually) cold Escabeche *es-ka-bEh-che*

Boiled or poached Hervido *er-vEE-do*

Steamed Cocido al vapor *co-thEE-do al va-pOr*

Ordering the Food

What do you recommend? ¿Qué me aconseja? *kEh me a-kon-sEh-Ha*

What is this, that? ¿Qué es esto(a), ese(a)? *kEh es Es-to(a), Eh-se(a)*

Is it meat or fish? ¿Es carne o pescado? *es kAr-ne o pes-kA-do*

Does it include garlic? ¿Lleva ajo? *lyEh-va A-Ho*

Some olives Una ración de aceitunas *OO-na ra-thyOn de a-theh-ee-tOO-nas*

May I change my order? ¿Puedo cambiar la orden? *pwEh-do kam-byAr la Or-den*

Can we have some more bread? Más pan, por favor. *mAs pAn, por fa-vOr*

Having a Drink

Spaniards make an occasion of pre-dinner drinking but, if you order white wine before dinner, like as not you will be brought sherry. Apart from beer and sherry, sweet drinks such as vermouth on ice or the *anís*-flavoured, brandy-like PACHARÁN are popular aperitifs. Gin is also served with sweet mixer-syrups. Mineral water or even GASEOSO, a fizzy lemonade, are used to dilute the wine.

At the end of the meal, both men and women enjoy sweet liqueurs. Ordering brandy (COÑAC), you will always be asked which you prefer: some are sweet and perfumed, others resemble French *cognacs*.

Ordering Drinks

We would like something to drink Quisieramos algo a beber *ki-sye-rA-mos Al-go a-be-bEr*

I (we) would like . . . Quisiera (quisieramos) . . . *ki-syEh-ra, ki-sye-rA-mos*

A glass of white wine Un vaso de vino blanco *oon bA-so de bEE-no blAn-ko*

A bottle of red wine Una botella de vino tinto *OOna bo-tEl-lya de bEE-no tEEn-to*

A half bottle Una media botella *OO-na mEh-dya bo-tEl-lya*

Red wine Tinto *tEEn-to*

Very light red Clarete *kla-rEh-te*

Rosé wine Rosado *ro-sAh-do*

White wine Blanco *blAn-ko*

Sparkling wine Cava *kA-va*

What do you recommend? ¿Qué me recomienda? *kEh me re-ko-myEn-da*

Can you recommend a local wine? ¿Puede usted recomendar un vino de la región? *pwEh-de oo-stEth re-ko-men-dAr oon bEE-no de la re-HyOn*

Non-alcoholic Drinks

Soft (cold) drinks Refrescos *re-frEs-kos*

Mineral water without (with) bubbles Agua mineral sin (con) gas *A-gwa mi-ne-rAl sEEn (kon) gAs*

Fruit juice Zumo de fruta *thOO-mo de frOO-ta*

Freshly-squeezed orange juice Un jugo de naranja natural *oon HOO-go de na-rAn-Ha na-too-rAl*

A fizzy lemonade Una limonada *OO-na li-mo-nA-da*

Iced water Agua helada *A-gwa eh-lA-da*

Tea with lemon, with milk Té con limón, con leche *tEh kon li-mOn, kon lEh-che*

Ordering Coffee

We would like coffee Quisieramos tomar café *ki-sye-rA-mos to-mAR ka-fEh*

Two small black coffees Dos cafés solos *dOs ka-fEhs sO-los*

Small coffee with milk Café cortado (corto) *ka-fEh kor-tA-do (kOr-to)*

Expresso coffee Café esprés *ka-fEh es-prEs*

Decaffeinated coffee Café descafeinado *ka-fEh des-ka-feh-i-nA-do*

Paying the Bill

You are unlikely to be hurried through your meal, and the bill will come only when you ask. Some places include service on the bill. If not, a 10 per cent tip is appreciated. The general rule is that tips get smaller as bills get larger: 5 per cent is about the minimum.

Leaving the Restaurant

May I have the bill, please? La cuenta, por favor *la kwEn-ta por fa-vOr*

Is service included? ¿El servicio está incluido? *el ser-vEE-thyo es-tA in-kloo-EE-do*

What is this charge? ¿Qué es esta cantidad? *kEh es es-tA kan-ti-dAd*

Tapas: *point out your choice*

Do you accept this credit card (travellers' cheques)? ¿Acepta usted esta tarjeta de crédito (cheques de viajero)? *a-thEp-ta oo-stEth es-ta tar-HEh-ta de krEh-di-to (chEh-kes de vya-HEh-ro)*

Thank you, this is for you Gracias, esto(a) es para usted. *grA-thias, Esto(a) es pA-ra oo-stEth*

We enjoyed it, thank you. Nos ha gustado, muchas gracias. *nOs a goo-stA-do mOO-chas grA-thias*

CHILDREN

Spanish children eat out in restaurants with their parents from their early years, and so they learn how to behave considerately. Children are welcomed everywhere except, perhaps, in the smartest of restaurants. The portions in Spain are enormous, so most small children eat off their mother's plate.

Finding food for children is not difficult, because the *tapas* dishes sold in bars are ideal for the young. Most children like CALAMARES (squid rings) which look vaguely like pasta, while dishes like meatballs in tomato sauce are universal. Don't be put off by sherry sauces – the cooking process destroys the alcohol. Fried fish is of better quality than elsewhere – with the ever-popular chips. *Hamburguesas* (hamburgers) are not recommended.

For breakfast try hot chocolate, for Spanish milk is homogenised and not particularly pleasant to drink. Nesquik is good for cold chocolate drinks.

Cafés and bars are open at lunch and before the late supper hours of Spain. However, it is preferable to feed children around 18.30 hours – not when bars are full of men having a drink after work.

Ordering in a Restaurant

A glass of orange juice Un vaso de zumo de naranja *oon vA-so de thOO-mo de na-rAn-Ha*

A bottle of fizzy lemonade Una botella de limonada *OO-na bo-tEl-lya de li-mo-nA-da*

Is it very spicy (hot)? ¿Es picante? *es pi-kAn-te*

A side order of potato chips, please Una ración de patatas fritas, por favor. *OO-na ra-thyOn de pa-tA-tas frEE-tas por fa-vOr*

Can you bring some (a few) serviettes? ¿Puede traernos (algunas) servilletas? *pwEh-de tra-Er-nos (al-gOO-nas) ser-vil-lyEh-tas*

Another plate, please Otro plato, por favor *O-tro plA-to por fa-vOr*

Some (two) spoons Unas (dos) cucharas *OO-nas (dos) koo-chA-ras*

Some teaspoons Unas cucharillas *OO-nas koo-cha-rEEl-lyas*

Where are the toilets? ¿Dónde están los servicios? *dOn-de es-tAn los ser-vEE-thios*

They are over there Están allí *es-tAn ah-lyEE*

Have you got a high chair, please? ¿Tiene una silla alta, por favor? *tyEh-ne OO-na sEEl-lya Al-ta por fa-vOr*

Please could you warm up the baby's bottle? ¿Puede calentar el biberón de bebé? *pwEh-de ka-lEn-tar el bi-be-rOn del be-bEh*

A half portion of . . ., please Una media ración de . . ., por favor *OO-na mEh-dya ra-thyOn de . . . por fa-vOr*

SPECIAL DIETS

Indicate your diet to the waiter and seek help.

Vegetarians

Spanish food is largely peasant cooking, based on good vegetables. Many restaurants have pictures of dishes outside. However, vegetarians should beware! Many soups, vegetable dishes and PAELLAS contain small amounts of bacon or sausage. There is also a tradition of cooking in pork fat. The only way to find out is to ask. Another thing to beware of is CUAJADA, which looks like yoghurt; it is junket, and so set with animal rennet (*cuaja*). Many pastries are, or used to be, made with lard.
A list of vegetables is given on pages 95–6.

Ordering Vegetarian Food

Do you have vegetarian dishes? ¿Tiene platos vegetarianos? *tyEh-ne plA-tos ve-He-ta-ryA-nos*
Is there any meat in it? ¿Hay carne en este plato? *A-ee kAr-ne en Es-te plA-to*
I'd prefer a salad Prefiero una ensalada *pre-fyEh-ro OO-na en-sa-lA-da*

Gluten-free Diet

Bread is the accompaniment to every Spanish meal, as meat, fish and poultry are normally served without vegetables. Ask for a side order of boiled potatoes (*un ración de patatas hervidas*) though it will be easier to get chips (*patatas fritas*). The good news is that there are many dishes that are not flour-based, particularly grills and rice.

Flour is used in wine-based sauces. Bread is commonly used in soups as a thickener, and is puréed for sauces, particularly those that contain nuts.
Among *tapas*, avoid the Basque *bola*, which is a béchamel-based croquette and all BUÑUELOS: many are based on choux pastry. Cocoa is sold mixed with a flour thickener.

Milk-free Diet

Milk has a low standing in the Spanish kitchen, being kept for young children. Cream is not much used either, except in the north. Avoid wine-cream sauces, but the majority of creamy puddings are based on eggs or ground almonds.

Choosing and Avoiding Foods

I have to keep to a diet Tengo régimen *tEn-go rEh-Hi-men*
I cannot eat flour (milk, sugar) No puedo comer harina (leche, azúcar) *no pwEh-do ko-mEr a-rEE-na, (lEh-che, a-thOO-kar)*
I am diabetic Soy diabético(a) *sOy dya-bEh-ti-ko*
I am allergic to mussels, (shellfish) Soy alérgico(a) a los mejillones (mariscos) *sOy a-lEr-Hi-ko a los me-Hil-lyO-nes (ma-rEEs-kos)*
I can't eat fried food No puedo comer los platos fritos *no pwEh-do ko-mEr los plA-tos frEE-tos*
I can't eat it, because I'm on a diet No puedo comerlo porque tengo régimen *no pwEh-do ko-mEr-lo por-kEh tEn-go rEh-Hi-men*

TIGHT BUDGET

You will be agreeably surprised at the cost of food and drink in Spain – from the price of gin to the cost of eating out. In the humbler places, a fiver will buy you a three-course meal with wine. Bars everywhere supply hot food – and a *ración* is enough for a main course. Much the same dishes are offered in restaurants of different categories. It makes sense, therefore, not to eat in cafés with a view – even if you choose to drink there. They are always more expensive.

Carafe wine (the house choice) is always cheaper than bottles. Drink it with mineral water – though many Spaniards cheerfully use *La Casera* (fizzy lemonade).

Water is now usually good and a jug of water with ice (*con hielo*) will cost nothing. At home, teach children to make drinks with real lemons (see recipe on page 113): cheaper and nicer than bought drinks.

Every eating establishment is obliged by law to offer a three-course meal with bread and wine for a set price – often very good value. Eat what others are eating, like the *plato del día* (dish of the day). Bean or vegetable dishes come as a course before the meat and can be very filling – enough for the meal in many cases. They can also be paired with soup or eggs, though these are all really alternatives.

Adapt to local food, rather than looking for what you eat at home. TORTILLAS are very filling and come with lots of variations. Fresh grilled sardines are cheaper than other fish and very good.

Avoid eating shellfish out – buy your prawns fresh in the market and cook them yourself.

Recipes in restaurants are very simple anyway. Give up beef – it is not always good in Spain; pork is a better choice.

You can also take advantage of the large Spanish portions to share salads or a starter. Fruit is cheaper than dessert and normally two fruits are brought. Out shopping, street markets are weekly in most towns and villages, and there are bargains if you are on holiday for more than a week.

Finally, make the most of your holiday to eat luxuries that are expensive at home. In Spain you can afford to buy avocados by the kilo, and strawberries and artichokes in season cost little. Gorge on oranges at 5 *pesetas* each, and wonderful tomatoes. These really are a bargain!

PRACTICAL TIPS

Self Catering

Your Spanish kitchen is unlikely to contain a teapot or egg cups. The pans will be different shapes from those at home, and it may well be easier to cook the Spanish way than to try and reproduce recipes from home without the proper equipment. Investigate your cooking facilities before you start shopping. Do you have a large *paella* pan, suitable for frying for a family? Do you have a casserole for vegetable dishes? And what about a lot of little brown oven dishes, called *cazuelitas*? They are ideal for individual baked dishes.

The tops of Spanish stoves are often very small, limiting you to two pans. Ovens are small too – and the butane gas type, which is common, has no regulator, only High and Low settings. Many Spaniards cook on the barbecue outside and this is both easy and fun. Deep frying may be easy, but it needs a lot of oil, which you may have to abandon when you leave.

What to Take

If you are self catering, it is worth taking your favourite knife. Take a pepper mill, too, as they are rarely supplied. Instant coffee is very expensive in Spain, but supermarkets stock most normal commodities.

Drinking Water

In public places drinking fountains are marked *agua potable* – don't drink from them otherwise. In some places tap water does not taste particularly nice and Spaniards drink bottled water at the table. If you do suspect the water, avoid eating lettuce that has been washed in it and make your ice cubes with mineral water.

Minor Illnesses

For upset tummies, induced by too much wine or fruit, kaolin tablets solidify things. For infections from bugs in water or food – far rarer than they used to be – Lomotil is very effective. Too much sun can also make you feel ill and Spanish chemists (*farmacía*) stock the normal aspirins etc.

What to Bring Back

Before you load your luggage with goodies such as *serrano* (raw ham) and salami-type sausages, make sure that Customs in your own country allow their import.

LANGUAGE

Useful Phrases

Greetings

Yes (no) Sí (no) *sEE (nO)*
Please Por favor *por fa-vOr*
Thank you (very much) (Muchas) gracias *mOO-chas grA-thias*
Hello (goodbye) Hola (adiós) *O-la, a-dyOs*
How are you? ¿Como está? *kO-mo es-tA*
Well, and you? Muy bien ¿Y usted (tú)? *mOOy byEn, EE oo-stEth, (too)*
My name is . . . Me llamo . . *me lyA-mo*
Delighted (to meet you) Encantado(a) *en-kan-tA-do(a)*
This is my wife (husband) Esta(e) es mi mujer (marido) *Es-ta(e) es mi moo-HEr (ma-rEE-do)*
Good morning Buenos días *bwEh-nos dEE-as*
Good evening (goodnight) Buenas tardes (noches) *bwEh-nas tAr-des (nO-ches)*
Tomorrow (in the morning) Mañana (por la mañana) *ma-nyA-na (por la ma-nyA-na)*
See you later (Till next time) Hasta la vista (luego) *As-ta la vEE-sta (lwEh-go)*

Buen apetito en España!

LANGUAGE

Questions and answers

What . . .? ¿Qué . . .? *kEh*

Why . . .? ¿Por qué . . .? *por kEh*

Which (pl) . . .? ¿Cuál (es) . . .? *kwAl es*

How . . .? ¿Cómo . . .? *KO-mo*

How long . . .? ¿Cuánto tiempo . . .? *kwAn-to tyEm-po*

How much (how many) . . .? ¿Cuánto (a, os, as) . . .? *kwAn-to (a, os, as)*

Where is (are) . . .? ¿Dónde está (están). . .? *dOn-de es-tA (es-tAn)*

Difficulties

Does it bother you(pl) if (I smoke)? ¿Les molesta, si (fumo)? *les mo-lEs-ta see fOO-mo*

Go away! Come back! !Vaya! !Vuelva! *vAh-ya, vwEl-va*

Excuse me (to get past) Perdóneme *per-dO-ne-me*

I am sorry Lo siento *lo syEn-to*

Can you help me? ¿Puede ayudarme? *pwEh-de a-yoo-dAr-me*

It doesn't matter No importa *no im-pOr-ta*

Money

I want to change some travellers' cheques Quisiera cambiar los cheques de viajero *ki-sYEh-ra kam-byAr los chE-kes de vya-HE-ro*

Can I pay with this credit card? ¿Se puede pagar con esta tarjeta de crédito? *se pwEh-de pa-gAr kon Es-ta tar-HEh-ta de krE-di-to*

Time

When does the shop shut? ¿Cuándo se cierra la tienda? *kwAn-do se thiEr-ra la tyEn-da*

Early, late Temprano (tarde) *tem-prA-no (tAr-de)*

Sometimes . . . A veces . . . *a vEh-thes*

Understanding Spanish

Could you say it again? ¿Puede volver a repetir? *pwEh-de vol-vEr a re-pe-tEEr*

I don't understand No comprendo *no kom-prEn-do*

Please speak more slowly ¿Puede hablar más despacio? *pwEh-de a-blAr mAs des-pA-thyo*

Please write it down Por favor, escríbalo *por fa-vOr es-krEE-ba-lo*

Do you speak English? ¿Hábla ingles? *A-bla in-glES*

Numerals

1 uno (una) *OO-no, OO-na*

2 dos *dOs*

3 tres *trEhs*

4 cuatro *kwA-tro*

5 cinco *thEEn-ko*

6 seis *sEh-is*

7 siete *syEh-te*

8 ocho *O-cho*

9 nueve *nwEh-ve*

10 diez *dyEth*

11 once *On-the*

12 doce *dO-the*

15 quince *kEEn-the*

20 veinte *vEh-in-te*

25 veinticinco *veh-in-ti-thEEn-ko*

30 treinta *trEh-in-ta*

40 cuarenta *kwa-rEn-ta*

50 cincuenta *thin-kwEnta*

60 sesenta *se-sEn-ta*

70 setenta *se-tEn-ta*

80 ochenta *o-chEn-ta*

90 noventa *no-vEn-ta*

100 cien (ciento) *thyEn (thyEn-to)*

150 ciento cincuenta *thyEn-to thin-kwEnta*

200 doscientos(as) *dos-thyEn-tos(as)*

300 trescientos(as) *tres-thyEn-tos(as)*

400 cuatrocientos(as) *kwa-tro-thyEn-tos(as)*

500 quinientos(as) *ki-nYen-tos(as)*

600 seiscientos(as) *sEh-is-thyEn-tos(as)*

700 setecientos(as)
se-te-thyEn-tos(as)
800 ochocientos(as)
o-cho-thyEn-tos(as)
900 novecientos(as)
no-ve-thyEn-tos(as)
1000 mil *mEEl*

Weights and Measures
Generous 2lb Un kilo
oon kEE-lo
1lb Medio kilo *MEh-dyo kEE-lo*

½lb Un cuarto kilo *oon kwAr-to kEE-lo*
¼lb Cien gramos *thyEn grA-mos*
1¾ pint milk Un litro de leche *oon lEE-tro de lEh-che*
17fl oz, generous ¾ pint Quinientos mililitros *ki-nyEn-tos mi-li-lEE-tros*
Half Medio *mEh-dyo*
Twice that Doble *dOh-ble*
A quarter Un cuarto *oon kwAr-to*
A dozen Una docena *oo-na do-thEh-na*

Hints on How to Pronounce Spanish.

1 Pronounce every letter, whatever its position in the word, eg leche (*lEh-che*). Exceptionally 'h' is always silent, as is 'u' in 'que' and 'qui'.
2 Accentuating the correct syllable is very important in Spanish. To help you, stressed vowels are in capitals in the imitated pronunciation, eg vino blanco (*bEE-no blAn-co*).
3 Spanish 'a' is pronounced like 'a' in 'father', but shorter; (and **not** as in 'hat' or 'hate') eg hasta mañana (*As-ta ma-nyA-na*).
4 Spanish 'e' is pronounced like 'e' in best or 'a' in 'Mary'; (and **not** as in 'he') eg bien (*byEn*), medio (*mEh-dyo*). 'er' is pronounced like Scottish 'er' in 'person', or like 'air' in English, eg supermercado (*soo-per-mer-kA-do*).
5 Spanish 'i' is pronounced like 'ee' in 'sheep', but shorter (and **not** as in 'right'). In the imitated pronunciation it is written as 'EE' if stressed, otherwise as 'i'. 'I' before another vowel is a short 'glide', written as 'y' in the imitated pronunciation, eg

si (*sEE*), pimienta (*pi-myEn-ta*).
6 Spanish 'o' is pronounced like 'o' in 'hot' (**not** as in 'low'), eg sopa (*sO-pa*).
7 Spanish 'u' is always pronounced as 'u' in 'pudding', eg fruta (*frOO-ta*).
8 Spanish 'r' is always strongly 'rolled', especially 'rr'. Children imitating an electric buzzer with the tip of their tongue come close to the correct sound.
9 Spanish 'z' and 'c' before 'e' and 'i' are pronounced like 'th' in 'thing', eg cien (*thyEn*), zumo (*thOO-mo*). In some parts of Spain and Latin America this sound is pronounced like an 's'.
10 Spanish 'j' and 'g' before an 'e' or an 'i' resemble the 'ch' in Scottish 'loch'. In the imitated pronunciation it is shown as a capital H, eg naranja (*na-rAn-Ha*).
11 'll' is pronounced like 'lli' in 'million', in some parts of Spain and Latin America like 'y' in 'yes', eg paella (*pa-El-lya*).
12 's' is always pronounced as in 'sing' (**not** as in 'rose').
13 Spanish 'v' is often heard as a 'b', 'd' as a 'th'.

CONVERSION TABLES

NOTES ON USING THE RECIPES

Weights and measures are written in metric and imperial. Follow only one set of measures as they are not interchangeable.

Abbreviations
Metric
g – gram or gramme
kg – kilogram
ml – millilitre
Imperial
oz – ounce
lb – pound
fl oz – fluid oz

Metric/Imperial Weight Conversions

50g/2oz	350g/12oz
75g/3oz	500g/1lb
100g/4oz	700g/1½lb
150g/5oz	1kg/2lb
175g/6oz	1.5kg/3lb
250g/8oz	2kg/4lb

Metric/Imperial Fluid Conversions
125ml/4fl oz
150ml/¼ pint (5fl oz)
175ml/6fl oz
200ml/7fl oz
300ml/½ pint (10fl oz)
500ml/18fl oz
600ml/1 pint (20fl oz)
750ml/1¼ pints
1 litre/1¾ pints
2 litres/3½ pints

Spoon Measures
Spoon measures refer to the standard measuring spoons and all quantities are level unless otherwise stated. **Do not** use table cutlery and serving spoons instead of measuring spoons as their capacity varies.
½ teaspoon – 2.5ml
1 teaspoon – 5ml
1 tablespoon – 15ml (3 teaspoons)

Oven Temperatures
The following settings are used in the recipes, providing centigrade, Fahrenheit and gas settings. However, cooking facilities in holiday accommodation may be limited or oven settings may be different or unreliable, therefore watch dishes carefully when baking in unfamiliar appliances.
110°C, 225°F, gas ¼
120°C, 250°F, gas ½
140°C, 275°F, gas 1
150°C, 300°F, gas 2
160°C, 325°F, gas 3
180°C, 350°F, gas 4
190°C, 375°F, gas 5
200°C, 400°F, gas 6
220°C, 425°F, gas 7
230°C, 450°F, gas 8
240°C, 475°F, gas 9

American Measures and Terms
Liquids: Imperial/American
8fl oz – 1 cup
16fl oz – 2 cups
20fl oz (1 pint) – 1 pint or 2½ cups
¼ pint – ⅔ cup
½ pint – ½ pint
Solids Whole pounds and fractions of a pound are used for some ingredients, such as butter, vegetables and meat. Cup measures are used for storecupboard foods, such as flour, sugar and rice. Butter is also measured by sticks.
Imperial/American
Butter – 8oz/1 cup (2 sticks)
Cheese, grated hard – 4oz/1 cup
Flour – 4oz/1 cup
Haricot beans, dried – 6oz/1 cup
Mushrooms, sliced – 8oz/2½ cups
Olives, whole – 4oz/1 cup
Parmesan cheese, grated –
1oz/3 tablespoons, 2oz/⅓ cup
Peas, shelled – 4oz/1 cup
Raisins – 6oz/1 cup
Rice (uncooked) – 8oz/1 cup

INDEX

Page numbers in italics refer to recipes

Alella 79
almonds 20, 21
Ampurdán 79
anchovies 21, 25, 63, *99-100*
Andalucía 7
Aragón 12-13, 78
artichokes 19, *100, 102-3*
asparagus 38, 51
Asturias 15-16
aubergines 24, 56

Balearic Isles 11
Basque country 14-15, 80
beans and pulses 20, 24, 38-9, 40, 41, 43, 45, 47, 43, 72, *101*
beef 24, 25, 29, 30, 32, 33, 37, 38, 48, 64, 67, 69, 71, 92
beer and lager 84
biscuits 20, 30, 51, 53, 55, 58, 71, 72
boar 45
brandies and liqueurs 83,84-5, 88
bread 25, 30, 37, 50, 54, 55, 70, 72
bream 24, 26, 31, 36, 52, 56, 68, 74
broad beans 43, 52
budget catering 121-2

cabbage 24, 33, 48
cafés and bars 115-16
cakes 19, 20, 24, 25-6, 35, 48, 49, 55-6, 60, 61, 66, 70-1, 72, 75
Cantabrican coast 14-15
capers 19, *110-11*
Castile 12
Catalunya 10-11
cavas 82, 84
charcuterie 30, 97
chard 17, 57
cheeses 26-7, 28, 29, 30, 45, 49, 50, 54, 56, 59, 62, 63, 64, 65, 67, 71, 72, 74, 95

chestnuts 30, 50, 59
chick-peas 24, 41, 72, *101*
chicken 33, 37, 46, 49, 57, 61, 92, *108-9*
children's food 120
chocolate 31, 84
cider 90
clams 20, 34, 53
coffee 84, 85
Condado de Huelva 80
confectionery 19, 25, 31, 43, 50, 56, 74
Costers de Segre 79
crab 29, 30, 53, 69
crayfish 29, 46
cuttlefish 31, 45, 68

dessert wines 82, 88, 89
desserts 22, 24, 31, 35, 36, 39, 42, 45, 46, 51, 53, 59, 70, 72, *112*
dried fruit 56
drinking water 83, 123
duck 56-7

eel 21, 34, 53
eggs 44, 45, 60, 64, 72, *98-9*
Extremadura 16, 80

festival food 114-15
fish, buying and cooking 93-5
fruit syrups 83
fruit and vegetables, buying 95-6

Galicia 15-16, 80
garlic 18, 19
goat 26, 59
goose 41, 54
grouper 31, 51
gurnard 21, 25, 66

haddock 36, 41
hake 28, 46, 51, 58, 59, 93-4, *105-6*
ham 45, 53, 55, 68, 73, 92, *102-3*
hare 46, 47
haricot beans 61
history of Spanish food and wine 5-6

ice-creams and sorbets 42, 43, *112*

jam 51
Jumilla 80
La Mancha 11-12, 79
lamb and mutton 27, 30, 32, 35, 36, 46, 55, 59, 71, 92
language (*see also* useful phrases) 125
lemonade 88, *113*
León 80-1
Levante 7, 10, 80
lobster 24, 42, 46, 47-8, 49, 67
lunches 117

mackerel 26, 38, 46
Madrid 11-12
map of Spain 8-9
meals and meal times 116, 117
meatballs 19, 25
meringues 51, 53, 68, 70
milk and cream 53, 87
mineral water 83
monkfish 62-3
Montilla-Moriles 80
mullet 29, 47, 53
mushrooms 25, 30-1, 44, 52, 53, 66, 68
mussels 50, 69

Navarra 12-13, 78
New Castile 11-12
nuts 20, 31, 23, 30, 50, 54, 59

octopus 62
offal 34, 35, 36, 44, 46, 47, 49, 51, 52, 56, 64, 68
oils and vinegars 17, 42, 75
Old Castile 12, 80-1
onions 27, 30
oranges 53
oysters 54

paella 21, 39, 54, *106-7*
partridge 37, 57-8
pasta 28-9, 39, 48

INDEX/ACKNOWLEDGEMENTS

pastries 28, 29, 30, 35, 41, 42, 54, 55, 58, 64, 65
pâtés and terrines 42, 56, 67
Penedès 78–9, 82
peppers 23, 52, 60, 64, 99–100, 108–9, 110–11
pheasant 39
picnics 97
pies and pasties 36, 55, 56
pigeon 59
pomfret 45, 55
pork 30, 32, 33, 46, 48, 55, 57, 60, 69, 73, 75, 92, 110–12
potatoes 19, 48, 56, 74, 100–1
prawns 29, 32, 41, 46, 94, 104–5, 107–8
Priorato 79

quail 33

rabbit 34
regional food 7–16
Ribera del Duero 81
rice 21–2, 66
Rioja 12, 76–8
Rueda 81

salads 20, 37–8, 43, 52, 55, 58, 60, 61, 62, 64, 75, 99–101
salmon 66
salted cod 18–19, 22, 23, 37, 42, 58, 62, 94
sangría 89, 113
sardines 21, 53, 68, 93
sauces 18, 19–21, 52, 57, 61, 65, 67
sausages 25, 26, 31–2, 36, 48, 53, 66, 69, 92–3
scallops 74
sea bass 48
self catering 122–3
shark 21, 27, 30, 50, 52, 53, 58, 65–6
sherry 81–2, 83, 86, 87, 88, 90
shopping for food 91–7
shops and stores 91–2
skate 64
snails 25, 29, 34
sole 17, 47
soups 18, 21–2, 25, 28, 34, 35, 39, 41–2, 43, 61, 62, 69–70, 75, 103–4
special diets 121
spices 38

squid 27, 31, 62
swordfish 36, 38, 58

tapas 116
Tarragona 79, 82
tea 87, 88, 90
Toro 81
tortillas 72–3, 98–9
tripe 28, 51
trout 64, 73
truffles 73–4
tuna 19, 23, 25, 50, 52, 56, 100–1
turbot 65
turkey 37, 57

useful phrases 123–5
    eating out 116–17, 118–20, 121
    shopping 91, 92, 93, 94–7
    special diets 121

Valdepeñas 79–80
Valencia 80
veal 32, 45, 71
vegetarian food 121
venison 32, 35, 74

wine regions 76–81
woodcock 24

The Automobile Association wishes to thank the following photographers and libraries for their assistance in the preparation of this book.

SPECTRUM COLOUR LIBRARY 5 Farmhouse, 10 Horse ploughing, 13 Pyrenees, 14 Fishing boats, 17 Olive trees, 22 Street market, 25 Lobster fisherman, 27 Goats on mountain, 28 Pavement restaurant, 31 Delicatessen, 34 Tapas, 37 Farming, Ibiza, 49 Fishermen, 52 Beehives, 65 Rural Mallorca, 77 Vineyard, 79

Fermentation jars, 82 Grapes, 85 Harvesting, 87 Gin bottles, 93, Fresh fish, 119 Tapas, 123 Café, Barcelona.

The remaining photographs are from the Automobile Association's own library (© AA Photo Library) with contributions from:

Jerry Edmundson, Eric Meacher, Andrew Molyneux, Jens Poulsen, Barrie Smith, Antony Souter and Peter Wilson.